# SHOW JUMPING
## *for* FUN OR GLORY

# SHOW JUMPING
## *for* FUN OR GLORY

### A Training Manual for
### Successful Show Jumping at All Levels

## ERNEST DILLON FBHS
## AND HELEN REVINGTON

PHOTOGRAPHS BY STEPHEN SPARKES

## KENILWORTH PRESS

Published in Great Britain by
Kenilworth Press Ltd
Addington, Buckingham, MK18 2JR

First published 2000

**British Library Cataloguing in Publication Data**
A catalogue record for this book is available from the British Library.

ISBN 1-872119-17-4

Layout and typesetting by Kenilworth Press
Line illustrations by Dianne Breeze

Printed in Hong Kong by Midas Printing Ltd

# Contents

*I would like to dedicate my book to those four-legged, long-suffering teachers who cannot speak for themselves — my horses. (Ernest Dillon)*

# *Foreword* *by Peter Charles*

Very few riders are naturally talented show jumpers; in fact, the majority of top show jumpers, even at international level, only remain at the top because of a strict regime of training and practice.

In modern show jumping a great deal of this training is conducted under the watchful eye of an experienced show jumping coach – a person whose knowledge, skill and experience help the rider to improve technique and maintain a high standard of horsemanship. The coach is also there to nip bad habits in the bud.

A good coach will have a well-thought-out system, based on experience in competition and knowledge of the physiology, biomechanics and psychology of horses and riders. His system will have proved itself time and time again as being progressive, consistent, easy to learn and easy to remember.

With good training, the rider will be able to nurture his horse's talent and ensure that his horse is always well prepared, mentally and physically, to cope with the increasing pressure of the competition circuit. He will also strive to progress up through the ranks, not content to rest on his laurels. A good coach will help his pupils to develop this positive mental attitude and will continually inspire them to better themselves.

All too often, in our highly technical age, we are tempted to over-theorise and over-complicate the schooling of horse and rider and tend to forget the essential basic building blocks of equitation. I was lucky enough to start my career with Iris Kellet, one of the world's most talented trainers. She steered me in the right direction from the very beginning and gave me a wonderful base from which to work and develop.

I have known Ernest Dillon for twenty years and I know that he is one of the gifted few who can cut straight through to the essentials without drama. He is direct and forthright in his approach, and he speaks the truth in simple terms; for those who listen and have the drive to succeed, this is a godsend.

Ernest's approach and techniques demand that riders work with their horses with a mind that accepts what it already knows to be true. He insists that horse and rider are comfortable and competent at one level before progressing to the next – whether they are working on the flat or over fences. This does not mean that his methods are boring – they are not; it just means that his pupils are successful!

Fundamental to Ernest is that the rider must have the courage to be alive with the horse and the track at every stride. The rider cannot be allowed to ride in a detached style but must be aware, and ready to adjust to and learn new ways. In this Ernest is rooted. From this solid base can be found the flexibility, motivation and confidence to try. We are, after all, never too old to learn.

This book gives down-to-earth, sound and sensible guidance to all aspiring show jumpers, whether they are just starting to learn to jump, are weekend riders jumping for fun, are frustrated riders trying to improve jumping technique, or talented enthusiasts seeking international glory. This book should not be in every show jumper's bookcase – it should be in every show jumper's hands!

Peter Charles

# Acknowledgements and Inspirations

Cyril and Dorothy Johnson FBHS, my first and best teachers.

Charlie Edwards, for providing me with all my best horses.

Robert Hall, dressage guru.

Elaine Straker, for believing in me.

Col. Joe Dudgeon, for directing my career.

Peter Charles, friend and one of the best riders in the world (also from Liverpool).

Fred Welch, for teaching me how to earn a living.

David Broome, the best male rider ever and a good friend.

Caroline Bradley, a great inspiration.

Liz Edgar, the most stylish and effective lady rider ever.

George Morris, great teacher and innovator.

Michel Robert, inspirational outlook on riding and coaching.

Rodrigo Pessoa, pure genius.

Ferdi Eilberg, dressage coach extraordinaire.

Bert de Nemethy, original thinker and lucid trainer.

Pat Manning, for her life-long help.

Bill Steinkraus, one of my idols.

Lars Sederholm, a trainer second to none.

Pat Burgess, I have borrowed some of her ideas.

Mark Phillips, for furthering my career.

Dick Stillwell, because he has always been there.

Most of all, Vicky, for putting up with me.

Ernest Dillon, FBHS

## ILLUSTRATION CREDITS

Line drawings by Dianne Breeze.
All photos by Stephen Sparkes and Helen Revington, except: page 11 (left) and 14 (left) by Bob Langrish.

## SPECIAL CREDITS

The authors would like to thank the following for their help with the photographs: John and Sue Nicol of the Headley Stud; Peter Charles; Perry Colgate; and Claire Bayman from West Wilts Equestrian Centre.

# CHAPTER 1

# Choosing the Right Coach

Training horses has to be an ongoing theme in every competitive horseman's life – from Olympic stars to those riding in local unaffiliated shows. There is no real end-product to training; it is not necessarily competing at a show or being able to jump higher or wider than anyone else in the fastest time. However, performing well at a show is the proof of good training. Thus, the best-trained horses will jump higher and wider in the fastest time, and, more importantly, with the least amount of wear and tear, so will inevitably win more competitions.

You should not be attempting to win classes at the beginning of your horse's career. His first few shows should be used only to familiarise him with various surfaces, ground conditions, types of show jump, the atmosphere, and the routine of a horse show. Mindlessly galloping around small show jumps time after time will not benefit you or your horse, nor can it truly be called show jumping.

Training of horse and rider should be an ongoing activity from which you should break off regularly, allowing time to compete. Competing will enable you to see if there is a weak link in your training programme; performing well at a show proves that your training is working, but there is always room for improvement.

Most horse and rider combinations that I teach are potentially much better than they imagine they are – all they need is direction and the right support. Through training, even the most seemingly talentless combinations have the opportunity to improve.

## The role of the coach

Being in everyday contact with their sport puts professional coaches in a good position to observe changes throughout it and to keep constantly up to date with changing coaching techniques. They will also be in a first-class position to see at first hand how the great riders tackle the everyday problems of correcting faults and, more importantly, avoiding them in the first place.

A good coach has to:
- Encourage the rider to ride a suitable and compatible horse.
- Have a well-thought-out system and be able to teach his training system in a clear and coherent manner.
- Be able to see all the facets of a given situation.
- Have patience.
- Give confidence.
- Push but not be too pushy.
- Eliminate stress, tension and confusion.
- Prioritise and create order.
- Teach riders to think fast, thus facilitating quick reactions.
- Find reasons not excuses.
- Accept responsibility.
- Create independence not reliance.

**Why train?** Whether you are in front of your horse's movement (1) or behind it (2), looking down over his shoulder (3) or back over his rump (4), you are not in balance with your horse. You are not moving in harmony with him and therefore cannot help him to leave poles up.

• Act as a sounding board for ideas and anxieties.
• Encourage the rider to be fit to train and ride.
• Have good communication skills – be able to explain his or her system clearly.
• Be constructive not destructive.
• Continually listen.
• Continually learn.

Coaches should not train to satisfy their own ego. When a pupil achieves success the coach may be able to bask in the reflected glory, but at the beginning the coach must allow the training to be a two-way interaction and he must be able to see his own shortcomings as well as those of his clients.

A good coach must be able to teach his system of work. Any coach who has not thought through a system will not coach well. Good, successful systems are based on experience, knowledge and an ability to focus on the horse and rider being taught. To me, 'focus' is the ability to see a complete, clear picture of the horse and rider. To see the clear picture completely you need a wide-angle lens. A narrow focus usually belongs to a narrow mind, and a coach with a narrow mind will miss important points; but what is achievable also depends a great deal on the talent and focus of the horse and rider. The coach with the widest-angle lens and the clearest picture in the world is still unable to produce miracles.

The coach must also be able to draw on his own

**David Broome**

❝At no time can you overlook the value of good training. Listen to everyone who has something positive to say and glean from it whatever you can. Never stop looking to improve. ❞

**Team spirit.** You, your horse and your coach should work together as a team.

experiences – both good and bad. Coaching should eliminate the trial-and-error factor by introducing a system proven to work through the coach's experience, success and knowledge. Knowledge is the accumulation of practical experience, observation, reading, intuition – and training.

A good coach is not only an innovator, but also an historian. The passing on of the right history is a great responsibility, but an objective view of less stylish, less correct and less effective methods are necessary for comparison.

'Responsibility' is another keyword for coaches. Initially the coach has to be responsible for goal setting, then he has to ensure that the goals are achievable and that they are achieved. Once the initial goals have been achieved it becomes a joint responsibility between pupil and coach to continue to set more ambitious but equally attainable goals. More than one goal should be set at a time – the achievable goal, such as being able to win the novice class at the local show in three months' time, and the ultimate goal, such as competing at Wembley's Horse of the Year Show, or perhaps at the All England Show Jumping Course at Hickstead. The ultimate goal should always be achievable – it is irresponsible to set an unattainable goal. Aiming too high leads to frustration and loss of confidence.

It is the responsibility of the coach to recognise the individual talents of each pupil – any talent a rider has is a gift he is born with and cannot be increased. When a rider can accept the extent of his talent, his or her frustrations will diminish. Most riders know, deep down, at what level they feel comfortable. Although talent itself cannot grow, a good coach can provide a rider with a system which will improve the chances of

success. Technique can be learnt and improved on, but natural talent can not; it can only be developed. Pushing riders too fast and too hard is not responsible. Accepting responsibility is also a skill that can be learnt, but accepting it and using it well is a heavy burden for the coach.

## Essential qualities for success

Both coach and rider have to be dedicated. Dedication is about having the absolute conviction that what you have chosen to do is the right thing for you and that it is a vocation you can stick to. I sometimes ask my riders 'Is there anything that would make you give up show jumping from choice?' They should have only one answer – 'No, nothing!'

Self-motivation, self-discipline, dedication and hard work are four major factors in ensuring a successful rider-coach combination. Self-motivation is essential in

**The result of good training.** A good coach can help you to attain your dream.

*Points to ponder...*
- *Work hard and get lucky.*

**Franke Sloothaak**

"The most important factor in success is discipline – without discipline you will go nowhere. You must get up every day and give your horse the work he needs. It is no good aimlessly ambling round the countryside or even around the schooling arena – you must have a constructive programme to train your horse.

Every horse is different and it is important that you are aware of what programme of training will benefit him most. It is always good to have the advice of an experienced coach who can look at you and your horse and can help you to construct the right programme."

training. If a rider does not have 100% conviction in working towards success then no amount of nagging and pushing will create success. Self-motivation is a huge part of any rider's talent and is essential to allow any coach to coach. Self-discipline is the partner of self-motivation. Nobody can discipline a coach or a thinking rider. An undisciplined coach will lead to an undis-

ciplined rider, but if the coach is self-disciplined and sticks to his chosen system, progress for coach, rider and horse should be smooth. Dedication means training to the limit through hail, rain and snow, fifty-two weeks a year. Dedication is hard work. Dedication is being able to see something through without taking short cuts and being able to pick yourself up after what appears to be a disaster. The road to success is paved with frustration and soaked with sweat and tears!

With training, success at any level can be very satisfying. My advice to you is: do what you can do well. Become stylish and skilful, train to the highest standards and buy the best horse you can afford. If you follow this advice you will develop the talent you have and be able to give your best.

# CHAPTER 2

# Choosing the Right Horse

My knowledge of what type of horse makes a good show jumper comes not from any great experience in the breeding industry but from my experience as a user and a trainer of the end-product. Over the years I have trained a great many horses and, without a doubt, the quick, sharp-witted, quality horse is the easiest type to train. I like a horse that is flexible in his body and prepared to use his character to work with me rather than against me.

It is a common misconception to think that if a horse is well bred he will have good conformation, and that if he has good conformation he will have good technique and movement. Unfortunately this is not always the case. Unless a horse has a severe conformational defect which is causing a fundamental weakness in his movement and which will become magnified under the stress of competition, then you must consider whether the horse is usable and for how long.

Some of the world's best horses have had defects that would not have passed a meticulous vet; one that springs to mind is David Broome's Mister Softee. He had sickle hocks, looked very weak in his hind legs and was very bandy from behind, but nevertheless he won an Olympic bronze medal in 1968 over one of the biggest show jumping courses ever seen; he was also three times European Champion. On the other hand I have spent many months trying to turn perfect-looking show horses into show jumpers with no success. There

was no apparent reason why these horses could not jump, but it was obvious that they did not have the enthusiasm or gutsy determination to try. Provided the quality comes out somewhere, whether it be in the stride, the jump or the brain, the old adage 'Handsome is as handsome does' rings true.

There are some structural defects that are likely to reduce the working life of a show jumper dramatically, and there are some features that I particularly look for when buying a horse. Here is a guide that may help you when choosing your show jumper.

A horse with severely upright pasterns will have less absorbency in his fetlock joints, so I do prefer a horse to have sloping pasterns. A large proportion of lameness in show jumping is caused by concussion and jarring of the feet and joints. Good feet are essential to allow for some expansion and movement; the old saying, 'No foot, no horse' holds a great deal of truth in it. When a horse lands over a jump all of his weight will come into one foot; that is, about 600kg of horse coming down onto an area of about 100cm$^2$, a huge amount of kilos per square cm.

A good, long, sloping shoulder is important. Straight shoulders cause more jarring, and straight-shouldered horses tend not to be very careful because of their inability to rotate the shoulder and bring it up in the correct way.

I tend to be attracted to horses with smallish heads that show quality, and a big 'bright and alive' eye is

**One in a million.** Milton had a style all his own – but it worked.

Stroller (at 14.2hh, a legend in his own lifetime) was the silver medallist in the Mexico Olympics and winner of the Hickstead Derby, yet he used to jump fences anyway he could and seldom the same way twice. Anglezarke jumped in a slightly inverted manner, with his head up and his neck hollow rather than rounded, but all of these horses shared one great quality – they had a burning desire to leave fences standing.

## The right horse for you

Many riders, when they go to buy a horse, have a good idea of what they want and of the type of horse they would like to ride in the ring, but unfortunately that horse may not be the most suitable type for them. What tends to happen is that they either find themselves over-horsed in terms of size or temperament, or just totally mismatched in terms of temperament, type and ability. It is difficult to tell someone who is just embarking on their show jumping career that suitability is one of the most important factors to take into consideration, not

**No foot, no horse.** On landing, all of the horse's (and the rider's) weight is taken by one foot.

important to me. I cannot buy a horse with what I can only describe as a dead eye – one that has no expression and looks asleep even when the horse is in work.

A well-muscled back of good proportions is great but I have no strict rules here – long- and short-backed horses have made superstar show jumpers throughout the sport's history, as have sway- and roach-backed horses. I cannot think of any great horses that have had cow-hocks or spavins, but I have already mentioned Mister Softee's sickle hocks, and the legendary Ryan's Son had large curbs.

Good and correct technique is also a point of much discussion between professional show jumpers. If you consider all the world-class horses and mark their technique out of ten against the classical description of a good jumper, none is likely to reach a perfect ten. Milton used to unfold his front legs in mid air and pushed his feet way out in front of him over the highest part of the jump. Classicists would dismiss him as being short of scope, saying that he was reaching for the back rail!

**Nick Skelton**

" You need a good horse – that's the most important thing. When you've got the best horse life becomes a lot easier, but good horses can be incredibly difficult to find. "

just finding a horse with a huge jump.

The other really important question to ask yourself *before* you buy a horse is: do you have the time, dedication and knowledge to do so? Horses are a twenty-four hour responsibility and if you are unsure whether you have sufficient commitment to carry this responsibility through, you should stick with the local riding school until you are sure.

Most people should start their show jumping career on a quality cob-type horse. This is not a big, thick-set, lumbering horse that people automatically imagine when the word 'cob' is mentioned. A Welsh Cob, crossed with a Thoroughbred or an Irish Draught x TB, would make a good type to begin with. He is likely to be alert enough and agile enough to go to the fence and jump correctly, but will be sensible enough not to rush or do other crazy things. This does not mean that with some years of experience you cannot upgrade to more quality horses with more scope.

Imagine going to Ascot or any other Thoroughbred Bloodstock Sales and buying yourself a horse straight off the racetrack, bringing it home and saying 'This is my new show jumper.' If you have little or no experience of training, or more particularly re-training, then you are going to dig yourself into a very deep hole. Young horses that have had a bad start or have been trained only to gallop are best left to the professional producers of horses, and even they will have a hard job with such horses; their success rate is very low.

What is important is that when you start out on your career you should not jump straight onto the kind of quality, athletic horse that you see jumping in the Olympics, the Derby at Hickstead or at the Horse of

the Year Show. To be honest if you *did* jump straight onto such a horse you would be more likely to scare yourself witless! If I were to present you with another Milton you would probably ask me to take him back within a week – not because he was not a good horse (he was probably the best, most multi-talented horse that has ever lived) but because he would not have been suitable for you. You would hardly recognise him as the equine genius he was with John Whitaker, not because you are a bad rider or him a bad horse but purely because you are not suited to one another. Good horses certainly do make good riders but, like a good husband or wife, they have to come along at the right time for you to take advantage of them.

At the beginning of my career I was lucky enough to have a very careful little horse called Davy Jones (shown overleaf). He had tremendous talent and used to hate hitting fences; the trouble was that, at the time, he was much better than I was. He came along too early in my career and neither of us fulfilled our potential together. We were both too young and too inexperienced to make a great partnership. Sure, we won quite a few classes together, but ... how I wish I had him now!

Ninety per cent of riders are recreational riders; they jump for fun and they try to get as much enjoyment out

---

**A useful prospect?** A Welsh x Thoroughbred, four-year-old. British native breeds crossed with Thoroughbreds often make good horses to start show jumping on.

'**How I wish I had him now**! The author and Davy Jones.

of show jumping as possible. To get that enjoyment they need a good-tempered, easy to train horse that is reliable and not too unpredictable. We do have to be realistic about the amount of scope and jump that we need. A high proportion of people who are looking for an international show jumper really need a top-class riding club horse or schoolmaster capable of jumping 3ft 6ins to 4ft (1.10–1.25m).

You and your coach should know at what stage you are at with your show jumping and you should have an idea, albeit a vague one, of how much talent and potential you really have. You may not always be the best judge of your own temperament, talent and progress but you should be able to assess yourself realistically.

Nearly everyone wants to spend as little money as possible. Prices of horses change from year to year and bargains can be found, but most people purely seek value for money. This is very simple to equate. If you pay an amount of money that you have judged to be reasonable and your horse successfully does the job that he has been bought for then he has proved to be value for money. If you pay the same amount of money and end up with a horse that does not do what you want, then you have not had value for money.

If you do not have a bottomless pit of money, or the sort of talent that it takes to jump international Grands Prix than you are looking for a happy, honest and fairly

brave little trier. If you are riding to a fence that you feel is big enough for you, and if you feel that your horse is wanting to get to that fence at least as much as you, and when you get there your horse clears the fence and lands in balance despite your usual number of missed or panicked strides, and he repeats this a dozen times and still feels happy it sounds like you have found just the right horse for you.

The show jumper's brain is a cocktail of courage and caution. The cocktail has to be mixed in the right strength so that whoever is drinking it can cope with its potency. Too much caution makes the horse too careful. He will not want to hit fences but if he does he will not want to try again. He will very quickly become stressed and will start stopping or napping and not wanting to go to the fence. The problem of having an over-careful horse can be overcome to a large extent by making sure that any competitions he enters are well within his scope and that he is ridden by a competent, accurate and experienced rider. He will need a lot of time and patience but the finished product will be a delight to ride and, having gained the confidence in his good rider, he will try over and over again.

Too much courage in a horse is not conducive to winning classes. Such horses do not disregard hitting fences but are sometimes unaware that they have. They appear to have an overdose of adrenaline, or perhaps, an insensitive mind. Often they seem much braver than they are because they appear happy to keep running at fences. Horses like these are difficult to win classes on, even with good jockeys, but brave horses ridden by novice riders can give the rider a great deal of confidence, even if the occasional fence comes down. There is nothing worse for the novice rider than to be eliminated at the first fence or to have a horse that is hiding in the corner, too afraid to come out and perform, or one that is jumping up and down on his back legs, refusing to go forward.

So the horse that most of us would like to obtain is something of a rarity: one that has a high degree of courage and a high degree of caution, one that is brave enough to go to his fences yet careful enough to jump them well and leave them up. This is not an impossible dream. If it were, then there would not be so many good show jumpers in the world today.

When it comes to finding the right horse for you, I

do not have all the answers, but what I can do is to point out some of the pitfalls you might encounter and advise you how best to steer around them. Over the years I have fallen into the snake-pit many times – every professional has (that is how most people become good judges of horses) – by buying and trying to ride a whole bunch of bad and unsuitable horses. Horses cannot help it if they have little or no talent, or if they are not as brave or as careful as they should be, any more than a person can help it if, through an unfortunate upbringing or lack of direction, they find themselves in the law courts too often or if they have two left feet when on a pair of skis.

## Buying your horse

Horses can be bought from breeders, dealers, high performance sales, bloodstock sales and local auctions, or by private sale. Most amateur riders buy their horses through advertisements in national magazines or local newspapers. Yet this can be the most time-consuming and frustrating way to buy your horse. Everybody within a 100-mile radius has got just the horse for you! It is the correct height, weight, colour, breeding and temperament. It is careful, scopey, and brave, has never stopped, has never napped, is easy to catch and has never shown the slightest inclination to bite, kick, buck, rear, weave, crib or box walk. In fact it does not need to jump water; this paragon of virtue can walk on it!

However, when you arrive to view the said paragon it is six inches shorter than stated and rushes at you with bare (but worn down) teeth, then turns on a sixpence, letting free both barrels before rushing off down a twenty-acre field never to be seen again! If you do manage to catch him and ride him, everything he does wrong, whether it be refusing, napping, rearing, bucking or knocking down fences will be '...the very first time he has ever done it'. How many times have I heard vendors state categorically, 'Honestly, he has never done that before today.' (I don't think!)

Another pitfall of buying through an advertisement is that you can never be sure who is doing the selling – whether it is the horse's owner, the owner's agent or an undisclosed dealer. The sale of horses is, to a certain extent, covered by the Trade Descriptions Act but should you need to resort to such means of redress the

**A rare find.** A horse who tries is worth his weight in gold.

procedures can be expensive, time-consuming, tedious and sometimes acrimonious.

You might decide that a young, unbroken horse is what you need. The inherent advantages are that so far nobody has taught it bad habits, training from scratch can be satisfying and rewarding, and it will tend to be cheaper than a horse already in work... but why? Simple – it takes months of hard toil and skilful training to produce a horse that is working well under saddle; and hard toil and skilful training cost money.

The disadvantage of buying a young, unbroken horse is you will have to put in all that work. If you do decide to buy a young horse, don't attempt to break it in unless you really do know what you're doing. My advice here is: seek professional help. Starting your horse off in the right way will, in the long run, save you money and lots of heartache and frustration.

Before you go to look at any horse, it is important to find out about the animal's past. Some useful questions to ask might be:
• How long has the present owner had him, and why is he for sale?
• How long has he been doing the job for which you intend to use him?
• What successes has he had?
• Has he hunted?

**Willi Melliger**

"Good horses are the important thing! I am on the look-out for good horses all the time, so I am lucky that as a dealer I get to see a great many horses. Yet, whether they are unproven youngsters or older horses that already have a good track record, the other important factor is how they feel to you. There is no point in riding a horse that does not give you a good feeling – if you do not like a horse that you are riding you are unlikely to succeed with it."

- Is he safe out hacking and on the roads, alone and in company?
- Is he good to box, shoe, clip, catch, and groom and with strangers such as the vet or the dentist?
- Is he suitable for the type of rider you are? Here, you have to be absolutely honest with yourself. If you are a nervous or novice rider you should tell the vendor.

If the horse you are going to view is registered with an affiliated body then you can obtain a record of his jumping successes. Check the record for long gaps and question the vendor about them – it is possible that the horse was either injured or went through 'a difficult spell'. All of this information can be gained via a telephone call and can save a lot of time.

Once you arrive to see the horse you need to give it a fair trial. Firstly you need to see him ridden by somebody else and then you need to ride him yourself. Never offer to get on straight away – an unknown horse is an unknown quantity and may be just waiting to get you off in any way he can. If the owner assures you that he is good in traffic, ask to see him ridden along the road – you could follow behind in a car.

As the horse is being bought for the purpose of show

jumping, try him over a large variety of fences. Put up double and treble combinations, as you are likely to jump them in competition. It is no good getting half way home and suddenly thinking that you should have tried this or done that. If the horse is being bought to event as well, make sure that you see him jump a couple of solid fences, taking a ditch or two and going through water. If he is very green he may have problems with these obstacles but you should be able to gauge his attitude and temperament.

If there are no such facilities at the vendor's home, ask him if he would mind taking the horse to a venue where there are plenty of coloured fences, including a water tray and solid fillers, to try the horse over, unless he is a young, inexperienced horse. The vendor may huff and puff but that is tough, it is your money and it is up to you to ensure that it is well spent. As long as you are fair to the vendor you are entitled to a good trial. On the other side of the coin it is completely unfair to waste people's time. As soon as you are sure that the horse will not suit you, say so – politely. It is very irritating to the vendor if you start picking holes in the horse – it may not suit you, but somebody will buy it and will probably be very happy to have done so.

Sometimes you may see the horse loose-schooled. If done in a professional manner this will give you a good idea of the horse's natural ability and will certainly tell you if the horse cannot jump. However, carried out by amateurs the whole process can quickly turn into a shambles. You may find yourself standing in the middle of the school and watching in bewilderment as the vendor tries to loose jump his young horse, who has obviously never been loose schooled before.

Of course, you should not offer to help because you cannot see the horse performing properly if you are running around waving your arms about – the real reason you do not offer to help is that you do not want to spoil the entertainment! But more seriously, this is not a good way to assess the horse's ability, and when you go into these yards and see this sort of thing happening it is nothing short of embarrassing.

Buying from dealers can be a very successful way of acquiring the horse you want. There will always be 'dodgy dealers', people who have a reputation for knocking poor or bad horses into shape and getting rid of them, but most dealers rely on having a good reputation and on getting business through return trade and recommendation. Good dealers seldom advertise so you need to hear about them through word of mouth.

Dealers may not know very much about the history of a horse but they are in the business of selling horses for profit and tend only to buy horses that they think are good enough to sell on in the first place. A dealer builds his reputation on selling the right horse to the right person, so he is unlikely to sell you a horse that he knows will not suit you. Some, but not many, good dealers will offer you a short trial period in which you may return and exchange the horse if you experience problems.

Some private vendors may also allow you to have the horse for a trial period, but this does require a huge act of faith on their part. They are taking a huge risk – there is no guarantee that the horse will return to them in the same condition that he left, and for the period that the horse is away no other potential buyer can view him.

If you wish to buy a horse from a sale you should ensure that he is sold under warranty – i.e. guaranteed by the vendor to be sound and free from vice. It can be quite useful to see several horses together so that you can compare their various merits and shortcomings and you can also control how much you spend – as long as you have strong self-will!

At high performance sales you can see horses ridden and jumped, usually by a professional rider, but at markets or auction sales access is usually very limited. You can look at the horse, feel his legs and gauge his temperament, and you may even be able to see him trotted up, but you are unlikely to be able to ride him or to see him gallop and jump.

If you are taking an adviser, make sure that he or she is working with you not against you. This may not be intentional but sometimes, through inexperience, they may put you off buying a horse that would suit you. You must be sure that your adviser is entirely familiar with your experience, ability and requirements, and also that the adviser has sufficient knowledge and experience to make a true and sensible judgement. Although you may have to pay for good advice from a professional person, you are far more likely to end up with the right horse for you than if you enter the minefield unaccompanied.

Whether you buy a horse from an open sale, a private vendor, a dealer or even from a friend, you should have him inspected by an equine veterinary surgeon. If you already use a vet in whom you have confidence then ask him to vet the horse for you. If the horse is a long distance away, ask him to recommend a vet to you in the horse's locality, ensuring it is not the same vet that already treats the vendor's horse.

Most veterinary practices will offer to perform either a full 'five stage' vetting or a 'part' vetting. A part vetting, although obviously cheaper than a full vetting, is usually little more than a visual observation of the horse standing and being trotted up in a straight line. It is really not worth the financial saving made. If you intend to insure the horse for loss of use then you must opt for the five-stage vetting. This is a very comprehensive vetting which takes about an hour and a half and includes the taking of blood. The blood is usually stored for six weeks but is not usually analysed unless you are worried that your horse was slipped an illicit substance at the time of purchase.

The perfect horse has yet to be born so tell the vet what you intend to do with the horse so that he can gauge whether or not any lumps, bumps or conformational defects the horse has are likely to affect his ability to perform for you. The important factor to remember about a vetting is that, ultimately, the horse needs to be usable only for the purpose you wish to use him for.

To sum up – make sure you see the horse stood up and trotted without tack; see him ridden on the flat and over fences which are a fair test of his honesty and ability before you ride him yourself. Try to be as objective in your opinion and judgement as possible and remember that first impressions are very valuable. If your gut feelings tell you that this is the horse for you, it probably is!

# CHAPTER 3

# *Lungeing the Show Jumper*

Many riders think of lungeing as a lazy alternative to riding – the 'I can't be bothered to ride today, I'll just give him half an hour on the lunge' syndrome – but correct lungeing can be a very useful tool for schooling the horse. I use the lunge primarily for two reasons; the first of these being to break down some of the resistances encountered while schooling, and the second to develop the horse's topline of muscles. It is very easy to lose your patience when you are sitting on your horse and he is not doing what you have told him to do, and I find the lunge is a better place to find a solution.

There may be any number of reasons *why* your horse is not doing what you want him to do, but to get into a big argument with him will get you nowhere. Sometimes horses will behave badly – and sometimes the answer is not to be found from on his back. It can be easier to get off your horse and see if you can solve your problems on the lunge. (This is not to say that every time you encounter a problem on your horse's back you should get off and lunge him instead, so that he has been allowed to get away with a disobedience, but if you feel that you are not going to solve the problem from the horse's back then by all means get off and see if you can solve it on the lunge.)

The only other reason I will use the lunge is for fittening work. You may not own a horse-walker or be able to ride your horse for as long as you would like and lungeing can 'top up' your horse's work level. You can teach a less experienced person to lunge your horse in an effective way, therefore releasing you from daily riding, although do realise that teaching a person to lunge in an effective manner does not equip them with the knowledge to *school* the horse on the lunge. Less damage is done by inexperienced people using the lunge than by inexperienced people trying to ride a fit competition horse.

The tack we use is very important. I came across a clear example of this a few years ago when a very prominent and world-renowned trainer was giving a lecture demonstration in front of a very large audience. He was intending to give an insight into his method of lungeing but was using a strange and, unbeknown to him, *young* horse. He tacked it up using a saddle, snaffle bridle and set of draw reins, all perfectly acceptable equipment to use on a horse that is known to you. Unfortunately, this particular young horse had a slightly suspect temper when it came to being restricted and the upshot was that the horse panicked, ran backwards, reared upwards and landed up in the laps of the audience. Thankfully, nobody was hurt in the incident, but the trainer and everybody watching learnt a very useful lesson: **know your horse before you do anything with him.**

The lunge line is much more effective if attached to the bit instead of a lungeing cavesson. I attach the line to the bit on the inside, lead it up over the horse's poll and thread it though the outside ring of the bit. This gives much more control over raucous horses, and a small amount of poll pressure encourages direct flexion. A lunge cavesson is good for use on young horses during starting. It puts no pressure on tender mouths and offers more control than a headcollar.

Schooling the horse well on the lunge is just as difficult as riding well, although it uses different skills. There are many different reins that you can use on the lunge but I use just three.

## The Chambon (see also Chapter 20)

The most useful and effective piece of equipment to use on the lunge is the Chambon. This device is designed purely for use on the lunge, and should never be used for riding as there is no quick-release mechanism. The Chambon is simplicity itself. It is attached, at one end, to the girth, then splits into two reins and comes up through the horse's front legs, and divides either side of the horse's neck. Each rein passes through rings either side of the horse's browband and is attached to a snaffle bit.

If the horse raises his head, gentle pressure is exerted on his poll and thus he is encouraged to develop a low head carriage. This allows him to stretch and bend though the whole topline of muscles and enables him to swing through his back. Your ultimate aim, when using the Chambon, is to have the horse's head and neck long and low – just above the ground. It is there not to force the horse into submission but to suggest by slight pressure that a rounded shape should be adopted.

The Chambon's value is that it encourages your horse to use his head and neck to balance himself by lowering the head towards the ground, and it develops a strong topline of muscles evenly on both sides. The horse releases himself through the back and can use his hind legs more effectively to propel himself forward actively. Once your horse has come to accept the Chambon he will work in a comfortable, relaxed way, swinging through his back and engaging his hocks evenly.

Even the horse with a low head carriage will benefit greatly from working in the Chambon. His ability to use his back will allow his hocks to come more underneath his body and redirect his balance to create a higher head carriage and a more controllable horse.

**Lungeing without a Chambon.** Note the horse's high head carriage and his lack of engagement. Lungeing in this manner does little to teach or strengthen the young horse.

To be of benefit the Chambon should be used on a regular basis. Younger horses should be lunged in a Chambon three times a week; some of my older horses are lunged in it every day – this is in addition to being ridden, not instead of being ridden. It is never necessary to use the Chambon for more than 25 minutes a day; younger horses need only 15–20 minutes.

When you tighten the Chambon ensure that you do so by small degrees. To increase the pressure on the poll

**Lungeing with a Chambon.** Note the horse's lowered head carriage, his rounded shape and how his hind leg is engaged and pushing him forward.

too quickly may panic your horse. As he feels the resistance he will try harder to raise his head, and as his anxiety increases he is likely to run backwards, possibly sitting down on his hind legs or falling over. This is why the Chambon should not be used when the horse is being ridden; there is no way that the rider can quickly release or slacken the rein.

Panic caused by the Chambon is rare as long as the horse is aware of what the rein does and that it is tightened gradually. I find that it usually takes six or seven periods on the lunge with the Chambon for horses to understand the rein's effect and for them to start dropping the head and working in a calm manner.

The result of lungeing in a Chambon, apart from stretching and creating flexibility, is that as long as the horse is kept active he will develop exactly the right muscles for show jumping. If you look at the shape of a horse using a Chambon you will see that he has his withers and shoulders up, his head and croup down, his hind legs pushing forward and his back as round as possible. Because there is never any direct pressure on the horse's mouth there is never an opportunity for the horse to lean on the rein or pull against the bit.

## Draw reins and side-reins (see also Chapter 20)

I prefer to use draw reins on the lunge rather than side-reins, my reason being that side-reins can be too inflexible and can set the horse's neck in a rigid, unmoveable position. Show jumpers need to be able to move and use their necks and backs up, down, and sideways. Flexibility and strength are two key words in the horse's physical development, and one without the other is of no use.

As with the Chambon, you should only tighten the reins slowly, noting your horse's reaction to the new sensation each time. If he looks a little worried, his ears start to go back, his head starts to shake or he becomes tense through the back, then go back a stage and loosen them off a hole. The aim is always to allow your horse to find his way in balance and outline, and for activity to be encouraged, not to force him into a specified shape and then chase after him. Submission to the rein is your primary objective – and if you gain that submission gradually, it will last a long time, but if you force the horse into submission, it will cause resentment and possibly panic. So using unreasonable pressure on your horse is counter-productive and will lead to major long-term problems.

I am not anti side-reins but I feel that they can be difficult to adjust and can create more problems when used badly than they can provide benefit when used well – and unfortunately I have seen them used badly all too often! As with all reins, the horse should move forward into the rein rather than the rein pulling the horse's head in; the result of which is that the horse soon finds a way of evading the pressure by dropping behind the bit and tucking his head into his chest. Eventually his brain will start to think backwards and he will not want to move forward at any time. Again adjust the reins slowly by degrees but always making progress.

# CHAPTER 4

# *Jumping Without a Rider*

Once your horse is happy and confident being lunged on the flat you can begin to think about the benefits of jumping on the lunge and loose jumping. The one thing that both lunge and loose jumping can do most definitely is tell you whether your horse cannot jump. It is very useful to observe your horse from the ground because you can see what technique he has and what part of that technique needs developing or correcting. For instance, if his shape is wrong over the fence you could lunge or loose jump him over wide, low oxers; or if he is a little careless you could loose jump him over some small, short-spaced gymnastic fences, one-stride doubles or even some small bounce fences. (For safe distances, see Chapter 12, Jumping Combinations.)

If your horse has been jumping badly when ridden but jumps beautifully when loose schooled take a careful look at yourself and your tack – something that is seemingly innocuous to you may be a source of severe discomfort to your horse.

Whether you are teaching a horse to jump loose or on the lunge you have a similar objective: that is, the horse should take care of himself and find his own bal-

ance without the interference of a rider. It is important that your horse is allowed to come into the fences without being chased so that he can approach them in his own tempo, whether it be in trot or canter.

When engaging in lunge jumping or loose jumping it is important to have an assistant to build and rebuild the jumps. (Tips on fence building are given in Chapter 8.)

## Loose jumping

Loose schooling will be difficult unless you can find an appropriate area in which to work. If you attempt to loose jump in a vast arena or school you will spend more of your time running after your horse than jumping him, and if your schooling area is too small your horse will be falling over himself trying to scramble around tight corners, jumping on his forehand.

However, if you do have an area of about 20m by 40m, loose jumping is a useful exercise for your horse. If the arena is outdoors you will need a substantial boundary fence. Any mirrors around the arena should be covered up so your horse is not tempted to run at them, thinking they are an extension of the arena. It is also useful to create a jumping lane to prevent your horse from turning round or running out. Of necessity the lane has to be constructed substantially higher than the fences to be jumped, but not so high that your horse can run out underneath it.

> *Points to ponder…*
> * *The way of progress and success is neither swift nor easy.*

**Jumping for fun!** A two-day old foal shows how easy it is.

The trick with loose jumping is not to chase your horse as fast as possible into a jump that is far too big for him to cope with. To have your horse crash into a jump, causing hurt, fear and loss of confidence, is the absolute opposite of what you want to achieve. Loose jumping is used to develop confidence and technique. It should be carried out in a controlled, calm and stress-free environment.

Another problem you may face is trying to find enough suitable people to help. Your assistants need to be fit enough to keep up, not aggressive or awkward, and need to be in the right place at the right time. Two assistants are ideal, one to send your horse on down the lane and one to keep him straight down the lane.

Ensure that your team knows where they should be and what their task is before you begin the schooling – that way the session will be constructive and is less likely to end in tears. When loose jumping make sure that you are always in the right place. If you are too far in front of the horse as he starts down the lane you are likely to head him off and he may turn back; yet if you are too far behind him you will seem to be in a chasing position and he will run away. It is important to keep on a line just behind the horse's hock and to use the lunge whip as a visual aid rather than a physical one.

Another good idea is to round the corners off with poles at about 3ft 3ins (1m) high. This will help the horse to run around the corners rather than into them, where he may stop and refuse to come out. Get your horse relaxed and used to running through the lane over

a pole on the ground. Progress from there is very straightforward as long as you do not frighten your horse by chasing, shouting, whip cracking and by building unsafe jumps. Remember to loose jump on both reins or you will develop a horse that can only jump off one leg.

The object is to teach the horse to think for himself and to promote good judgement and self-preservation, not to see how high or how wide your horse is capable of jumping. It is of benefit only as long as your horse's confidence is maintained. There is nothing more beautiful than a horse jumping free over a substantial fence, but it is not necessary or useful to turn a loose-jumping session into a puissance competition. I cringe when I hear people boasting that their three-year-old can jump an oxer 5ft 3ins (1.60m) high and 6ft 6ins (2m) wide – just how many jumps has a horse got in his life, and what is the point of wasting those jumps for vanity's sake?

## Lunge jumping

I prefer to see horses jumping well on the lunge rather than loose. As I have said, you need a great deal of skill to lunge on the flat and you need extra skills to lunge a horse over a fence. The whole set-up for lunge jumping is important – just as important as the set-up for loose jumping. You must make sure that the lunge line cannot get caught or snagged on anything, causing the horse to receive a nasty jerk in the mouth. I use the lunge line as

**Easy does it.** A youngster's first introduction to jumping on the lunge.

**Loose jumping.** A young stallion by Carnival Drum loose jumps with confidence and scope.

described before, threaded from bit ring to bit ring over the poll, giving more control. This also means that you have to be very careful not to catch your horse in the mouth at any time, especially mid-jump. If you do he may become inverted or start to turn mid-air and lose his balance.

You need to ensure that your horse cannot run past the jump, either on the outside or through the inside, so I use running rails on both sides of the jump. The wing on the inside of the jump needs to be low enough that you can easily let the lunge line slip up over the running rail and over the wing without you having to fling your arm and the lunge line into the air. The maximum

height for an inside wing would be 3ft 3ins (1.30m). 'Jumpkins' or 'Blocs' are excellent substitutes for a traditional wing, although with Blocs it is handy to fill them with sand or gravel so that they are not easy to knock over. Running rails need to cover any place where the lunge line might snag.

Both lunge jumping and loose jumping should be used sparingly and only on good going, never on sticky, slippery or hard going as this will destroy rather than build confidence. If you use these forms of jumping to *help* your schooling rather than to *replace* it, then both you and your horse will reap the benefits.

# CHAPTER 5

# The Rider's Position

At the beginning of the twentieth century Federico Caprilli, an Italian cavalry officer, watched the new wave of flat-race jockeys and realised that this method of riding would benefit the jumping horse. Up to this time riders were encouraged to lean back as the horse took off to lighten the load on the forehand. Caprilli devised a method of riding over fences which allowed the horse enough freedom to negotiate the obstacle with as little interference as possible. The very simple basis of this system was that if the rider's centre of balance remained over the horse's centre of balance, the horse would have more freedom of movement and thus be able to clear much higher and wider obstacles without endangering either himself or his rider.

To achieve an effective, balanced position you should fulfil the following criteria:

• You should remain in balance with the horse throughout the approach, take-off, flight, landing and recovery phases of the jump.

• You should remain independent of the rein and under no circumstance interfere with the horse's mouth over the jump.

• Your upper body should remain still and not distract the horse with any sudden or unnecessary movement.

• Your lower leg should remain close to the horse's side, strong and immobile throughout the jump.

• Your weight should be light on the horse's back.

If you are not sitting correctly on your horse you will never be successful. The foundation of the modern jumping seat is a strong lower leg. Without a strong lower leg it does not matter how you sit because as soon as the horse moves you will lose your position. The lower leg has to stay in the correct position while you are taking off, in the air, and when landing. That is not to say that it cannot move a couple of inches backwards – there are very few riders who can maintain an absolutely perfect position throughout the jump, and there are several riders at the top of the tree whose legs do slip back but this does not stop them from being very effective riders.

Years ago, if you could hold a £5 note between your knee and the saddle as you rode then your position was considered to be nigh on perfect. However, if you clamp your knee to the saddle, the knee acts as a pivot, causing the lower leg to swing backwards and the upper body to swing forwards. This puts the rider's weight onto the horse's shoulders, making him heavy on his forehand – not good when you need your show jumper to be light on his forehand with all his power generating from his hindquarters.

## The light, balanced seat

The light, balanced seat allows the rider always to remain in balance with his horse. The main elements of this position are:

The correct position for flat work.

The correct position for jumping.

- The lower leg should be underneath the rider with the stirrup leather vertical.
- The knee, which used to be firmly clamped to the horse's side, is now more relaxed and can be held slightly off the saddle to enable the lower leg to be kept close to the horse's side.
- The toes, which were once expected to be turned to the front and parallel with the horse's side, should now be positioned at about five to one.
- The heel should always remain lower than the toe.
- It is the angles of the rider's hip, knee and ankle joints which allow the rider to find a point of balance whilst the horse is in motion.
- You should keep your head up, with your eyes looking where you are going. Your head is the heaviest and least flexible part of your body: if your head drops forward or to one side it starts to influence the balance

of the rest of your body, and thus the balance of the horse.
- You should try to ride with your back as straight as possible. If you allow your back to sag the rest of your body becomes weak, which will affect your ability to control your horse. If you are in a good position in the saddle you are in a good position to control your horse; a good maxim to remember is: 'Erectness without stiffness, suppleness without slackness.'

The above will give you the solid foundation for a light, balanced jumping position and help to maintain a strong and well-balanced seat over fences.

Of course, your position in the saddle should change if you are working your horse on the flat, and for this I would probably let my stirrups down two holes. Do bear in mind, though, that schooling jumping horses on the flat is **not** the same as schooling dressage horses.

The type of horse you are riding, combined with experience and personal preference, will govern whether you should sit lightly on, or up out of, the saddle on the approach to a fence. I teach riders to adopt the light, balanced, forward seat as an exercise at any level and especially when they first come to me for training. I firmly believe that riders learn to ride better when they are taking their weight in the forward position, out of the saddle, and then develop the position in the saddle at a later stage if that becomes necessary. It develops their sense of balance and rhythm without having to use their seat at all. Consider that both flat-race jockeys and National Hunt jockeys complete their entire 'round' without their seat ever touching the saddle, and observe their wonderful sense of balance and rhythm. As the horse moves underneath the jockey, the jockey shifts his weight to remain in balance with the horse.

There is no absolute formula for the forward seat and different horses respond to different weight distribution. In some cases the seat may be just a quarter of an inch (less than 1cm) out of the saddle, whereas in others the horse will go better if the seat is a full 6ins (15cm) out of the saddle.

There are many exercises that we can do to assist the forward seat and to improve the rider's balance. Working a rider on the lunge allows the rider to work with no reins and no stirrups and helps to develop a sense of balance and position.(See photos opposite.)

**Rob Hoekstra**

❝ It is really important to remember the basics. Position is everything in any form of equestrian sport. You need to have a good position to be able to control your horse; to make him go forward, to stop and to go left or go right at exactly the right time. Position is everything! ❞

The most common mistake that riders make nowadays is to ride with their stirrups too long. Up to a point, the shorter your stirrups, the easier it is to find a point of balance. (See illustrations below.). A good guide is that the angle of your knee should be at approximately 90 degrees.

## The hands

The hands should be carried just above the withers. Some horses need to be ridden on a longer rein; some riders need to ride with a longer rein. If you a have a short arm it is very difficult to ride with a short rein! The position of the rider's hands has to correspond

Correct stirrup length and effective leg position – note that the stirrup leathers are vertical

Short stirrups = a strong centre of balance

If you ride with long stirrups your body is more likely to pivot out of balance

**Lungeing exercise.** During your first lunge lessons without stirrups or reins, you may feel more secure if you hold the pommel with one hand. Here the rider rotates one arm in a full circle, and then the other.

**Lungeing exercise.** This exercise will help your posture and encourage you to look straight ahead.

**Lungeing exercise.** This exercise will help you to adopt an independent jumping position.

**Lungeing exercise.** This will not only improve your jumping position but also your flexibility.

**Crest release.** The crest release gives the horse freedom throughout the jump whilst allowing the rider to remain in control.

with the conformation of both the horse and the rider. The hand, through the rein, can be used in three different ways:

- **the direct pulling rein**, in which the hand and elbow are being drawn back to the body;
- **the open rein,** in which the hand is moved away from the horse's neck – a good rein to use on a young horse and in a jump-off situation to ask the horse to start to turn in the air over a fence; and
- **the indirect rein**, in which the hand is actually going across the horse's neck – there is little use in the sport of show jumping for the indirect rein but it can be used to encourage an increase in the left or right flexion of the horse's neck.

At this point it is a good idea to give you some advice about what to do with your hands when the horse is jumping. The easiest concept to understand, and perhaps the most straightforward to learn, is the '**crest release**' (shown above). This can be a **long** release, a **short** release or an **automatic** release.

- In the **long release** the rider puts his hands on the neck of the horse some 9ins to 1ft (approximately 23–30cm) in front of the horse's withers, the action

of the release enables the novice rider's horse to jump without hindrance and the rider to remain in balance using the horse's crest to stay in position.

- The **short release** is the same as the long one, but the hand moves forward only 3–4ins (7.5–10cm). This technique is used by riders who are a bit more advanced.
- When the rider is in perfect balance he will use the **automatic release,** which simply means that he will automatically follow the movement of the horse's head and neck throughout the jump with a soft arm and elbow.

## Weight, balance and stillness

As you should be aware by now, how you distribute your weight on top of your horse will greatly affect his way of going. The essential thing is that your weight should be evenly distributed in front of and behind your knee (fifty per cent in front, and fifty per cent behind). Too much weight to the fore of the knee will make you top heavy, throwing your horse onto his forehand; too much weight behind the knee and you will get left behind, making you hang on to your horse's mouth to keep your balance. (See illustrations overleaf.)

Balance, during riding, is not static but dynamic. Because the horse is always moving and shifting his balance it is important that you follow his motion and do not get left behind. If your hips and shoulders are already in a good position, the balanced seat allows you to be still on take-off – **no extra movement is necessary.**

In jump riding one of your aims is to keep your body movement down to a bare minimum. This has two functions. The less movement you make, the more able your horse will be to listen to the movement you do make, so that he will be better equipped to respond to your aids. I liken this to two people talking to each other. If they are in a room on their own they can talk quietly and each person will hear every word that the other says. If they are at a party with loud music and other people chatting around them they not only have to shout but each is likely to miss words. Try, in your riding, to keep the 'background noise' down to a minimum. The second reason for keeping your movement

The rider who tips forward will put too much weight on the horse's shoulder and forehand. He will also have an unstable lower leg. This rider will be unable to create power through the horse's hindquarters.

This rider is in balance. His weight travels directly down his spine, through his seat and stable lower leg, into his heel.

The rider who tips backwards puts too much weight onto his horse's loins. He will tend to get left behind his horse's motion as the horse moves off. This rider would eventually cause his horse to become stiff and resistant through the jaw, neck, shoulder and spine.

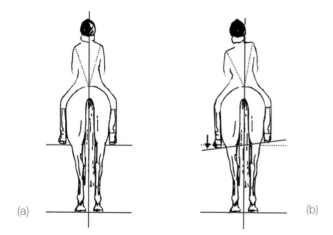

(a) (b)

(a) The correctly balanced and positioned rider puts his weight centrally in the saddle and equally into the stirrups.

(b) The rider who is out of balance will throw his horse out of balance because the weight is unevenly distributed over the horse's back. His horse will, in time, become sore and stiff. In this illustration the stiffness will particularly affect the near side, where most of the rider's weight is deposited.

to the minimum is to prevent your horse from being thrown off balance by your sudden shifts of weight.

As I have pointed out, if you are already in the forward position your position when jumping a fence should, in principle, remain the same through approach, take-off, landing and when moving away after the fence. If you are approaching the fence in a sitting position you will need to move into the forward position as you take off, but you should not throw your weight forward as this will only put your horse off balance and onto his forehand, the cardinal sin of show jumping.

Once you are in the correct position your muscles should stay firm and in place but soft. It is not desirable for your muscles to be tight and hard. Riding with your muscles tight all the time will make you and your horse tense and stiff and will seriously impair your enjoyment of riding and your horse's enjoyment of carrying you. There should be no tightness in your back or your shoulders. When sitting into the saddle in canter or sitting trot it is important to allow your hips to open and close with the movement of the horse – this needs loose, relaxed muscles. If your position in the saddle is strong yet soft you will be able to let your horse move and rise underneath you. As a result he will be free to use his shoulders and will not be thrown off balance by changes in your weight. A strong, soft position will allow your horse the freedom to perform well and give you the confidence to ride well.

**Position is everything.**

# CHAPTER 6

# Basic Work on the Flat

Working your horse on the flat is a vital part of his education and is essential if you want to keep him fit and in good health, and wish to prolong his jumping career. As a rider you must learn how to get your horse working at his most efficient. You need to be able to ride your horse forward, in a straight and calm manner, under control and with the ability to start, stop and turn without resistance.

Your horse needs to be as supple and as strong as his bodily structure will allow if he is to perform at his best in the show jumping arena. Fundamentally the horse is a herd-grazing animal and is prey rather than predator. His strongest instinct, along with feeding and reproduction, is that of flight – to go as fast as possible in a straight line – flexibility does not come into it, nor for that matter, does jumping! Horses are not inherently supple creatures and the most supple horse in the world will never be as flexible through its body as the most inflexible cat. However, through regular schooling on the flat, you can vastly improve your horse's suppleness.

Most show jumping riders initially think that working on the flat is tedious and they just want to get on with the jumping, but firstly, it does not have to be boring, and secondly, a horse will not jump well without a strong foundation of work on the flat.

Work on the flat for the show jumper is very different from pure dressage. In show jumping the two primary aids are the legs and the hands; in dressage, through riding with much longer stirrups and a deeper seat, the seat also becomes a primary aid. The seat and weight of the rider do have an influence in show jumping but are mainly an influence of balance not of direct control.

## OBJECTIVES

So let me define your immediate objectives in terms of control. Your ultimate aim when schooling a show jumper is to create an athlete that:

- can perform at his peak for a short period;
- is instantly obedient to his rider's aids;
- is infinitely adjustable;
- can alter his way of going at the merest indication from his rider;
- has the strength and flexibility to leave all the fences standing in a faster time than all his rivals; and
- can do all these things as calmly as possible.

To start with, you need to be able to start, stop, go left or right and to concentrate on your horse's **RIBS** – his **Rhythm**, his **Impulsion**, his **Balance** and his **Speed**.

Do not set yourself a timescale when you are train-

*Points to ponder...*

- *Whips and spurs are aids not crutches.*

ing a horse, but **do** set aside enough time to train. If you set time targets you are likely to become disappointed and tense, as will your horse. The same is likely to happen if you have not set aside enough time for each schooling session. I always tell myself: 'It will take five years to train this horse properly.' In fact it takes less time – usually twelve months to two years – but if I were to set out with the idea that, 'I'm going to school this horse in five months', it would probably take forever as I would become impatient and frustrated.

Also remember that no horse works at 100% efficiency – ever! If you can keep your horse's attention and feel him concentrating while he tries to get things right for you, you should feel that you are winning. Listen to your horse: he will tell you how to ride him. If he suddenly starts to rebel against what you are asking him to do, stop and ask yourself why. Is he becoming mentally or physically tired? Does he understand what you are asking him to do? Is he mentally and physically ready to do what you are asking? Is what you are asking him to do hurting him? – his muscles may ache, just as yours do when you try out a new exercise.

So, returning to your list of objectives, you need your horse to go forward, stop, turn left and turn right – sounds easy, doesn't it? However, the show jumper has to do each of these tasks at the **instant** at which he is told to do so. If your horse starts to turn five metres after you ask him to, he will probably miss the next jump altogether. Worse, you will panic and pull your horse off balance.

## Moving off the leg ...

The first thing the horse must learn is that when we close the leg on his sides he **must** move forward. So, you ask your horse to walk on by squeezing him with your legs, but he does not move forward. What do you do? In order to connect with your horse's brain, you have to use your knowledge of his flight instinct to make him move forward. Ask him to walk on again, using the leg just as lightly, but this time back the leg up with a sharp smack with the whip at the same time. This time he will jump forward – you must expect him to do this and be careful to move with him and not to catch his mouth with the bit. This doesn't sound very pleasant but you should only ever need to do it once or

**Di Lampard**

" I still have help with my riding. When I am riding on the flat, let alone jumping, I can only feel what my horse is doing. I need someone on the ground to see what the horse is doing. By feeling what the horse is doing and by being told what he is doing I can put the two together to initiate improvement. "

twice before your horse learns to move instantly off the leg. The idea is that eventually you are able to use less rather than more leg to get a correct response from your horse. It is kinder that the horse learns obedience right from the beginning of his career than to have to be retrained at a later date.

One school of thought dictates that the rider wears spurs, and that if a squeeze with the leg does not produce a response then the spur itself should be used to move the horse forward. In my experience very few riders are skilled enough to notice the subtle difference between riding with the heel parallel to the horse's side with an inactive spur and riding with the heel towards the horse's side employing the spur. For this reason I prefer to see riders using the whip to back up the leg until the leg position is firmly established.

## ... and stopping

Now that you have your horse moving forward you need to be able to stop him. Unlike pure dressage trainers I believe that you should be able to stop your horse with the bit and the reins alone, rather than with the combined aid of your seat. In the arena it is vital that your horse responds quickly to any change of contact on the rein, but again this comes only with training. Bear in mind, though, that the show jumping horse is naturally stronger than the average hack, so your normal contact needs to be quite clearly defined and may, at times, be quite strong. It is quite acceptable to have a reasonably strong contact with your horse's mouth as

**The halt.** A resistant, unbalanced halt.

**The halt.** A good, square halt.

long as you can still ask him to slow down or speed up without him becoming out of control. If a small amount of increased pressure is not enough to stop your horse then a more assertive hold needs to be taken until he comes to a halt or decreases his pace as you have asked.

It is important that you think of your lower arm as an extension of the rein, so that your lower arm can act as a shock-absorber between your body and the horse's mouth. Imagine that your reins end at the elbow and not at your hand. If your elbow is too floppy, it will create an uneven contact between the hand and the bit leading to irregular pressure on the horse's mouth, eventually causing your horse to become headachy and uneven in his gait as the discomfort increases. If your elbow is too stiff and clamped to your side, it will not absorb any discrepancy between your hand and your horse's mouth. Your arm needs to be elastic in order to take up the movement between your body and the rein

*Points to ponder…*

* *Nothing can pull against nothing, so don't pull.*

– it is important that your hand remains still to the horse's head, not still to your own body, so that the contact between hand and bit remains constant.

## The half-halt

The only tool that we have to teach the horse obedience to the rein is the transition. We have to develop the 'half-halt' transition so that it becomes a natural indicator to the horse that the rider is about to ask for a change of pace, tempo or direction.

I do not like the expression 'half-halt' as it is not possible to have half a halt, but it is the only term we have in equestrian vocabulary to describe the way we contain the horse's energy prior to change. What we are actually trying to do is to condense the horse's stride for a brief moment, and in that moment the horse has to engage his hocks, bring his forehand up a little and make himself compact.

The effectiveness of the half-halt depends on having an instantaneous response to the leg and rein aid. To teach your horse to half-halt you must first teach him to halt. The halt does not have to be square or the outline round as it does in dressage, but it does have to happen when you ask for it. Make as many walk–to–halt/

halt–to–walk transitions as it takes for your horse to learn that he must perform each transition as soon as you ask. Then progress to trot–to–halt/halt–to–trot and canter–to–halt/halt–to–canter transitions. Remember: the horse should move briskly away from the leg each time.

Once your horse can perform these transitions well return to walk–halt transitions and progressively reduce the amount of time you spend in halt until the halt occurs for just a fraction of a second before you send him forward again. Now repeat the exercise in trot and canter. Each time you ask for the halt your horse should feel, for a moment, like a compressed spring waiting to be let free – when he feels like this, you have perfected the half-halt.

As you try to progress you will probably find that your horse has a seemingly endless repertoire of evasions. Whether he twists his head, puts his tongue over the bit, crosses his jaw, throws his head up or down, your reaction must be the same. Do not lose your temper, just continue to use the correct aids. Eventually he will hit on the idea that it is easier to do as he is told than it is to evade. It may take you several months to develop a consistently satisfactory half-halt but, once you do, you have the foundation for success.

## Adjusting the stride

It is important that the show jumping horse learns to become infinitely adjustable. To effect this, you need to use your leg and rein aids, and half-halts, as described above. Practise increasing and decreasing the tempo for short periods of five or six strides in trot and canter, making sure that the horse does not 'get away' from you. Quicken the stride rather than lengthen it so that you have a feeling of it going 'up tempo' rather than becoming long and flat. Now try lengthening and shortening the stride. Again, do not lose control or a fight will ensue while you try to regain it. Practise between two landmarks and see how many variations of stride patterns you can make, lengthening and shortening, quickening and slowing down. Eventually you will have a gamut of variations within your horse's gait.

## Turning

Good turns are at the foundation of good jumping. When you work your horse on the flat you have to make sure that he turns precisely where you want. This is up to you. You have to start thinking about the turn way ahead, and you need to begin creating the bend

**Adjusting the stride.** A strong, lengthened canter.

**Adjusting the stride.** An equally strong collected canter.

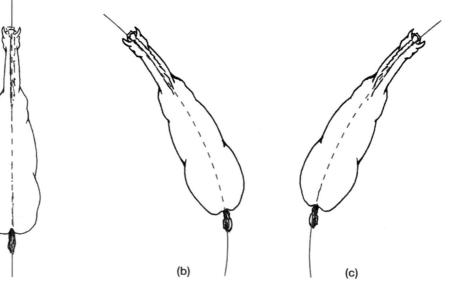

## The aids for a correct bend

• **The active diagonal** – the outside rein **(1)** and the inside leg **(2)**. The outside rein controls the horse's rhythm and pace and limits the amount of bend. It also affects his balance and carriage. The inside leg is the driving aid. By nudging the horse's side with the inside leg (using a momentary increase in pressure, not a flap) the horse is encouraged to bend around it. Once the horse has responded to the nudge by bending correctly, stop giving the aid and allow the inside leg to remain firmly against the horse's side, encouraging him to continue to bend around the leg.

• **The passive diagonal** – the inside rein **(3)** and the outside leg **(4)**. The inside rein supports the bending aid of the inside leg. The inside rein should not be pulled back – this will cause too much bend in the neck or a tilting of the horse's head. The outside leg prevents the quarters from swinging out. It is positioned 4–5ins (10–12cm) behind the girth. During sideways movements the outside leg may be used as a driving leg to promote forward, impulsive movement.

• **The rider's weight.** When asking for bend the inside hip **(5)** should carry fractionally more weight.

possibly five metres before the turn physically begins. If your horse is supple and is flexing in the direction of the required turn, he will automatically bend more easily (see illustration below).

Each hand and each leg has a specific job. The outside rein is the most important because it is this rein that controls the horse. The horse's natural instinct is to travel towards the outside rein and if we encourage him to do so we can control his energy. By using your inside leg to push your horse's inside hind leg towards the outside rein, you can create a situation in which the control of your horse is very definitely in your outside rein. The inside rein can create the bend in the horse's body corresponding to the arc of the circle. The outside leg is used to prevent the horse from falling out of that arc. The most common rider fault when making a turn is to pull on the inside rein and to drop the outside rein – result: the horse falls out through the outside shoulder.

Once you begin to turn your horse onto a circle, you will begin to feel how balanced or – more likely – how unbalanced he is. A young horse learns to balance himself naturally, but once in training he needs to relearn to balance, carrying his rider. Just like us, horses are right- or left-handed and will therefore find it easier to perform in one direction than another. It is your job to teach your horse to feel equally balanced on either rein.

If your horse feels unbalanced while walking or trot-

## Straightness and bending

A truly straight horse **(a)** is able to bend his body equally to the left **(b)** and the right **(c)**.

(a)　　　　　　　　　(b)　　　　　　　　(c)

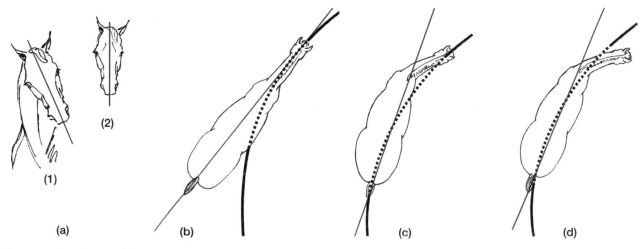

**Common bending problems.**

**(a)** The horse tilts his head (1), either to the outside – or more commonly – to the inside. Caused by pulling on the rein. Solution: decrease pressure on the pulling hand, use both legs to drive horse forward and straight; head will return to correct position (2).

**(b)** The horse avoids bending his body by swinging his quarters out. Solution: lighten the inside rein, use outside leg and outside rein to prevent quarters from swinging out; strengthen inside leg to encourage horse to wrap around it.

**(c)** the horse avoids bending his body by letting his outside shoulder bulge outwards. Solution: use outside rein to prevent outward drift and lighten contact on the inside rein; ask the horse to move onto a straight line so that you can straighten his shoulder and neck before asking for bend again.

**(d)** The horse avoids bending his body by excessively bending his neck. Solution: increase pressure on the outside, controlling rein, and increase pressure on the inside, controlling leg; do not 'let go' of the inside, supporting rein. Frequent changes of direction will reduce the likelihood of the horse learning to avoid the bend.

---

ting in a circle he will either 'fall in', that is he leans to the inside, putting too much weight on his inside shoulder and allowing his hindquarters to come off the true bend; or he will 'fall out', that is he allows his outside shoulder (or whole body) to come off the correct bend towards the outside.

Bending is more than just having the skill to turn or make the horse look in the right direction. It is the fundamental and basic tool for making all the interconnecting parts of the horse more efficient. Every time you bend a horse in one direction, you are stretching the opposite side of the horse and developing the flexibility which enables the jumping horse to operate over wide obstacles. It also enables the horse to shorten with the right degree of impulsion and to maintain perfect balance. It important to remember that flexion is possible without bend, but bend is not possible without flexion.

Often the side of the horse that bends more easily to the inside can be the more difficult side. This is the side the horse finds more difficult to stretch, so he 'curls up' around the inside. Horses that have this habit must be encouraged initially to be straight and then to develop equal flexibility on both sides.

## Creating impulsion

There is a world of difference between a horse that is slopping around at any pace and a horse that is moving and thinking 'forward'. Your horse should feel full of impulsion and bounce, whether he is walking, trotting or cantering. To obtain this feeling it is necessary to contain your horse between rein and leg aids. By keeping your legs firmly on his sides and by controlling excessive forward movement with your reins, your horse should begin to feel athletic with a spring in his step.

Think of a ball: the more air or pressure that is used to inflate the ball the higher it will bounce and yet all that pressure is kept contained inside the ball by its shell. If there is a hole in the ball the energy will escape and the ball will become flat, much as your horse will if you

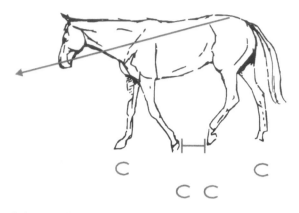

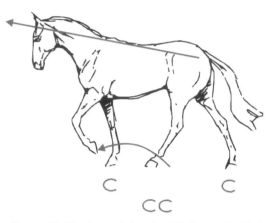

**A lazy walk.** The horse is in a 'downhill' shape; he is not engaging his hindquarters, therefore he is not 'tracking up'.

**An active walk.** The horse is in a 'uphill' shape; his hindquarters are engaged and pushing his hind leg forwards powerfully. He is, therefore, 'tracking up' – his hind hoof is placed in front of the track left by the front hoof.

cannot contain him between rein and leg. As a rider you must learn to put pressure on your horse until he is bouncing ... but remember – if you put too much pressure into a ball it will burst!

In general, grass roots riders will be seen chasing their horses along, trying to make them go faster, when in fact they are really only succeeding in making them flat. The best way to improve your horse's forwardness is to keep practising the exercises we have discussed for making your horse more responsive. Changes of tempo and length of stride will increase your horse's awareness of your aids, and half-halts will help to collect him, making his paces rounder and stronger.

The importance of all of this work is that it will enable you to:

(a) ride your horse at a correct speed to jump the fence;

(b) stay in balance at that speed;

(c) maintain that speed in a rhythm; and

(d) create enough power to jump the fence.

**A young horse showing a loose, balanced trot.** In time this horse will learn to use his hindquarters more strongly. Lunge work with a Chambon can help to encourage engagement.

# CHAPTER 7

# More Advanced Work on the Flat

Riders who do not recognise that their horse is ready to move from one stage in their development to another tend to make their horses stiffer and weaker, becoming inverted and set in the jaw. So once your horse is moving forward in an energetic manner you can begin to increase his flexibility by introducing him to lateral work.

Most of the time we ride a horse forward, asking him to work in a straight line, lengthening and shortening the stride, increasing and decreasing the tempo and, whilst this may increase his agility and balance, it does little to improve his flexibility. Now here comes one of life's big paradoxes – a horse cannot be absolutely straight until he is truly able to bend. In other words, for a horse to be able to move well in a straight line he must have supple limbs. How do we achieve supple limbs? By asking the horse to bend.

I do not feel that the half-pass serves a particularly useful purpose when training the show jumper as it is terribly difficult to teach, but I do like my horses to be able to perform shoulder-in, leg-yield, rein-back and travers (quarters in). Sounds technical? Well, let me explain.

First, we need to go through some of the jargon used in lateral work. For argument's sake we will assume that you are working in an enclosed arena with two long sides, two short sides and, therefore, four corners. So that you can easily follow the exercises, we will also assume that your arena is 40 metres long on the 'long' side and 20 metres wide on the 'short' side, just like a standard dressage arena (see illustration overleaf), with markers to guide you. Unless I talk about a circle at the centre of the arena (between B and M) you can assume that a circle commences at A or C.

When working on the 'outside track' you are working as near to the outside rails as is practically and safely possible – don't break your foot just because you are hugging the outside rails! The 'inside track', technically, can be anywhere between the outside rails and the halfway line of your arena, but more often the term is used to describe an invisible line about 1–2 metres in from the 'outside track'. When you work your horse on the flat try to work him on the inside track and down the centre line as often as you do on the outside track so that he does not become dependent on the rails for staying 'straight'.

Horses are often described as working on two, three or four tracks. This alludes to where your horse places his feet:

- If he is working on two tracks, his hind feet will travel along the same line as his front feet.
- If he is working on three tracks, his near fore will move on one line, his off fore and near hind will move on a second, and his off hind will move on a third.
- If he is working on four tracks, his near fore will be moving on one line, his off fore on a second, his near hind on a third, and his off hind on a fourth – easily

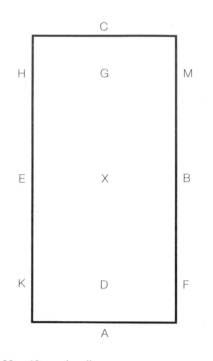

Standard 20 x 40m schooling area.

on his circle before you attempt to go straight. Whether he is working on three or four tracks, if he is running out through his outside shoulder, he is falling to the outside and not performing a shoulder-in. In other words he is going sideways with a stiff, resistant spine rather than moving forwards with a supple, flexing one. The essential part of the shoulder-in is that your horse's weight is carried by his inside hind leg and that he is pushing himself sideways via that hind leg rather than loading his weight onto his outside shoulder, in which case he is dragging himself along.

As your horse becomes more proficient, you can ask for shoulder-in at any point, e.g. on a straight line whilst out on a hack.

The aids are pretty much uniform in all the exercises we do. Your inside leg is used to bring the inside hind leg of your horse underneath him to push him forward – creating energy. Your outside leg is preventing his quarters from swinging out – controlling the energy. Your inside rein is used to position your horse's shoulder off the outside track: once your horse is in position the inside rein becomes light, purely maintaining posi-

done unintentionally if your horse is very excitable, but much more difficult to achieve on purpose!

## The shoulder-in

I use the shoulder-in as the basic lateral exercise for the show jumper. In shoulder-in, your horse keeps his hindquarters on the outside track whilst his body bends evenly so that his front legs are on the inside track. It is not an exercise in which you are trying to gain points but one in which you are encouraging your horse to move through his inside hind leg and through his shoulder without losing his balance. One way of picturing the shoulder-in is to imagine that you are riding a 20-metre circle with a correct, even, bend throughout your horse's body and that as you come off that 20-metre circle onto the long side you maintain that same bend even though you are travelling in a straight line, on three or four tracks depending on the stage in the horse's training (this is explained below).

Putting imagination into practice, the most important thing to remember before you start to ask for a shoulder-in is that your horse must be absolutely in balance

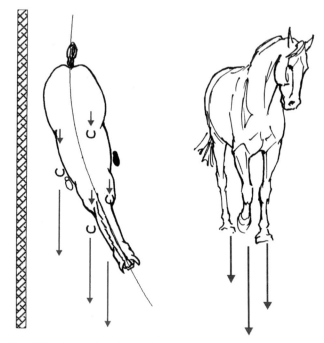

**Shoulder-in.** In shoulder-in the horse's body becomes equally curved throughout its entire length. In this diagram the shoulder-in is being performed on three tracks. Remember that your active leg should be supported by your passive leg.

tion, whilst the outside rein, which your horse is moving towards, controls his energy and power. The angle of the shoulder-in depends entirely on the stage of your horse's schooling, as he becomes more advanced the angle of shoulder-in can become more acute, progressing from three to four tracks. A very slight amount of flexion is often called 'shoulder-fore' rather than shoulder-in. You should begin your shoulder-in at walk and when this feels well established you can progress to trot.

## The leg-yield

In leg-yield the horse moves forwards and sideways at the same time, crossing his front and hind legs. Your horse's outside leg provides the power for the movement, stepping sideways before the inside leg moves across in front of it. It is an exercise I use a lot because I feel that any schooling movement that makes a horse cross his legs is beneficial.

To explain the exercise, let's assume that you are walking in a clockwise direction on a 20-metre circle between C and X, in good balance. At present your inside (right) leg is driving your horse's inside hind leg to the outside of the circle, your outside (left) leg is preventing him from falling out, your inside (right) rein is positioning him on the circle and your outside (left) rein is controlling him as he moves towards it. At M you begin to move diagonally across the school towards K. As you do so your outside (left) leg becomes the inside leg as you drive the horse's outside leg across the arena, and the right leg, previously the inside 'driving' leg becomes the outside 'controlling' leg, ensuring that the quarters do not fall out. The right rein becomes the controlling rein and the left rein maintains the straightness of the horse.

The sideways action of your horse can be as steep or as shallow as you wish. As he becomes well established in lateral work he may be able to leg-yield from (for example) K to B, but initially you should aim to travel from K to M or literally from corner to corner. It is important that your horse's body should remain in a relatively straight line because if you allow him to bend excessively through the neck he will begin to fall through the shoulders. A small amount of bend away from the leg aid is acceptable to begin with, but your ultimate aim is to have the horse's spine straight and his legs crossing. If you were to take this exercise a stage further you would begin to create a bend towards your leg aid; this is known as half-pass – it takes a long time

**Leg yield.** In leg yield, whether carried out across the diagonal (far left) or along the side of the arena (middle), the horse's body remains straight whilst his legs cross. His neck may bend slightly to the outside. The horse moves away from the active outside leg. The passive inside leg should support the active leg, controlling the horse's hindquarters.

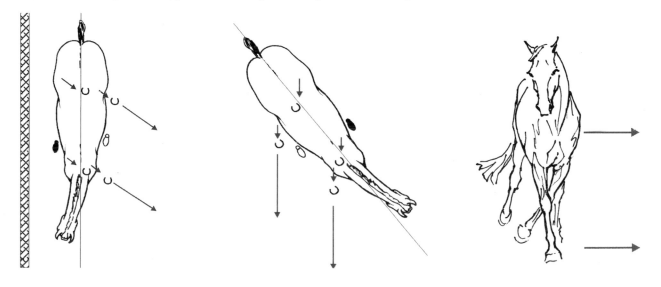

to achieve, and is not an exercise I teach my riders very often.

As with the shoulder-in, once you have perfected the exercise at walk you can progress to riding it at trot, but one of the most important points to remember with both these movements is that it is better to ride a small angle well, with good control, balance and rhythm, than it is to ride an acute angle badly.

## The rein-back

The rein-back is a very important exercise. Unlike the walk which has four beats, the rein-back has two beats – it is a sort of trot in reverse, without a moment of suspension. It increases your horse's flexibility through his spine and hind leg joints, puts power into his hocks before he moves forwards and also demonstrates that he is fully submissive and obedient. When your horse is totally submissive to the rein-back he is much easier to control. Imagine that when you ask your horse to rein back he lifts his head, crosses his jaw, hollows his back, and either will not move or goes sideways. Now multiply that feeling by one hundred and see yourself approaching a fence and trying to ask your horse to slow down. Disconcerting, isn't it? If your horse is not submissive to all your rein and leg aids then this will begin to happen.

The rein-back is not a natural movement for the horse and at first he will find it quite difficult – in fact it begins by being a 'trick' and eventually evolves into a correct movement. To move backwards he must tilt his pelvis and raise his back, not easy – especially with the weight of a rider on board. I teach my horses to rein back even before I get on them, in the stable and at the long-reining stage. If a young horse learns to go backwards firstly at a voice command and then with the voice command backed up by the rein aid it will make the job far easier when you get on top.

To teach your horse to rein back when ridden it is easier if you have an assistant on the ground to help you. To begin, position your legs slightly behind the girth to prevent your horse from moving sideways; then ride him quietly forward with your legs into an unyielding hand. As your horse can't move forward (because your hands prevent that), nor can he move sideways (because your legs prevent that), he will learn

*Points to ponder...*

• *Give one aid, get one response.*

to move backwards from the leg aid. To give him the idea, your assistant can gently tap the horse's shins with a dressage whip while you back up the aids with a verbal command of 'back'. Continue practising the exercise until your horse is moving backwards confidently in a straight manner, and then attempt the rein-back on your own. Never force the movement and only ever ask for four or five strides of rein-back at a time, as continually repeating the movement will put strain on your horse's joints.

Once you have perfected the rein-back you can begin to use it as a tool to improve your horse's paces. Teach your horse to walk, trot and canter immediately from the rein-back, and also teach him to walk forward a couple of strides, rein-back, trot forward five strides, rein-back, walk forwards three strides, rein-back, etc. etc. This 'rocking' not only helps your horse to engage his hocks but also sharpens his mind and teaches him not to anticipate. Ninety-nine per cent of your job as a show jumper is to get your horse's weight onto his hind legs and off his front legs so that he is light in front and active behind. Our aim, at the end of the day, is to get one stride right – the take-off stride. If your horse has all his power in his hind legs and his front end is light he can push himself over the fence.

## The travers

The travers or quarters-in is the most advanced lateral exercise that I teach to the show jumping horse. As with all lateral exercises its purpose is to engage the horse's hindquarters and to increase his flexibility. Basically, travers is a half-pass with the horse's head on the outside track, bent in the direction of the movement, and the horse's quarters on the inside track. In this exercise it is the horse's outside leg moving across in front of the inside leg that provides the impulsion.

What you must avoid is blocking the action of one leg with the other. So if you are trying to create activity with the inside leg and to push the horse away from the wall with the outside leg you may find yourself in a situation where your inside leg, asking for impulsion, is blocking the action of the outside leg, asking for the bend. So your inside leg must create enough power and activity as you come off the corner of the arena to be able just to rest against your horse's side as he moves into travers on the long side of the arena.

The action of your outside leg is exaggerated; it is not just controlling your horse's quarters but manipulating them, bending the quarters inwards. The inside leg is still creating activity, the inside rein is still bending and the outside rein is still controlling.

## Improving the canter

The canter consists of a series of bounds and is the gait that show jumping horses use for jumping. Therefore it is the gait that you have to perfect if you want to show jump well – or at all. When cantering 'true' your horse should canter in a three-time beat: the outside hind leg strikes off first (first beat), then the inside hind leg and outside fore leg move together (second beat), and the

off fore, the leading leg, should follow (third beat) before a moment of suspension. You should not be able to hear four hoof beats during the canter – this is a sign of lack of impulsion and that the hind legs are not engaged but are running to keep up!

In the **counter-canter,** or 'false' canter (which is not something that I would normally teach the show jumping horse as an exercise) the horse canters with a right lead on a left-hand circle or with a left lead on a right-hand circle.

I only ever use the counter-canter to help a horse that is particularly stiff on one rein or the other. The important thing to remember with counter canter is to control your horse's quarters, because if you allow his quarters to swing in he will become 'disunited': that is the leading foreleg is on the opposite side to the leading hind leg. This is not only very uncomfortable for the rider but also very unbalancing for the horse – and he would not be able to make a good jump from a disunited canter.

To show jump well the horse must be well trained, must be in balance, must be infinitely adjustable and must have a good canter. The action of jumping is purely an exaggerated canter stride, therefore if your horse's canter is powerful and in balance so will his jump be.

A horse that is well trained and infinitely adjustable has to be in complete balance or self-carriage whilst maintaining power without your help. He has to maintain this self-carriage each time you ask him to increase or decrease his length or speed of stride so that he can remain in balance at all times.

## Useful exercises

One of the exercises I do to improve the canter is to construct a 20-metre square on the ground using poles. At each of the four corners of the square I place a cone about 5 metres in from the poles. Start by trotting your horse between the poles and the cones and when he

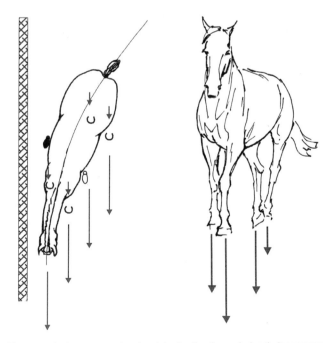

**Travers.** In travers, as in shoulder-in, the horse's body becomes equally curved throughout its entire length. In this diagram the travers is being performed on three tracks. Remember that your active leg should be supported by your passive leg.

*Points to ponder...*
- *Absolutely refuse to carry the horse.*

**The cones and poles exercise to improve the canter.** Trotting around the cones and inside the poles will encourage your horse to bend around the corner evenly. Once he is balanced throughout the exercise in trot you can progress to canter, but do remember to ride the exercise in both directions (on both reins).

feels confident at trot progress to canter. When he is trotting and cantering around the square in good balance you can reduce the square to 15 metres and bring the cones closer to the corners. At each corner your horse has to take a powerful stride with his inside hind leg to propel himself around the bend. As the square becomes smaller and the angle of the corner more acute, his weight is taken completely by that leg.

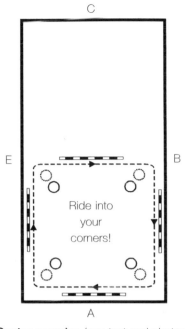

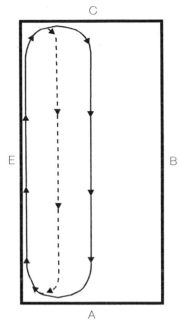

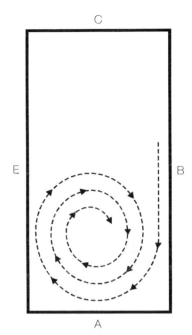

**Canter exercise** (see text and photos opposite). Trot and then canter between the poles and cones. As you get better, move the cones nearer to the corners.

**Canter exercise.** Concentrate on riding balanced, round bends and straight lines in between.

**Canter exercise.** Canter in decreasing and increasing circles. Work on both reins equally. Can you manage a 5m circle?

(See illustrations on facing page and above.)

Another exercise to improve the canter uses the long side of your arena. Canter your horse along the long side of the arena and then as you reach the corner turn him on a 10-metre half circle and canter down the centre line. As you reach the end of the arena turn again on a 10-metre half circle to the outside track. Each time you complete the turn keep the canter straight on the long side. As your horse's canter and balance improves you can reduce the half circle to 5 metres (see diagram above).

Spiralling in from a 20-metre circle down to a 10-metre circle and out again to a 20-metre circle is also an excellent canter exercise. Again, you can eventually reduce the inward spiral to a 5-metre circle as your horse's canter improves. (This exercise is shown above.)

An exercise which is useful to prevent your horse from falling in to his corners is to canter him along the short side of the arena, halt, turn into the wall and to canter back along the short side. Concentrate on creating a powerful halt–to–canter transition.

A trotting exercise to improve your horse's bend and balance is to trot along the long side and at the corner of the arena begin a 10-metre circle but as you reach the centre line, having completed a half circle, move diagonally back to the outside track, trotting back to the next corner to repeat the exercise (see diagram overleaf). Concentrate on creating correct bends and straightness.

## The flying change

All show jumpers need to be able to do flying changes. The flying change required for show jumping is more utilitarian, forward-going and less collected than the change required in a dressage test. Its purpose is to allow the horse to change direction fluently at canter during a show jumping round. You do not have time in the arena to stop, change leg and start again so it is important that the horse is on the correct lead when going around a corner toward a fence to maintain all the other qualities of the canter that we have discussed.

I like to teach my horses the flying change in

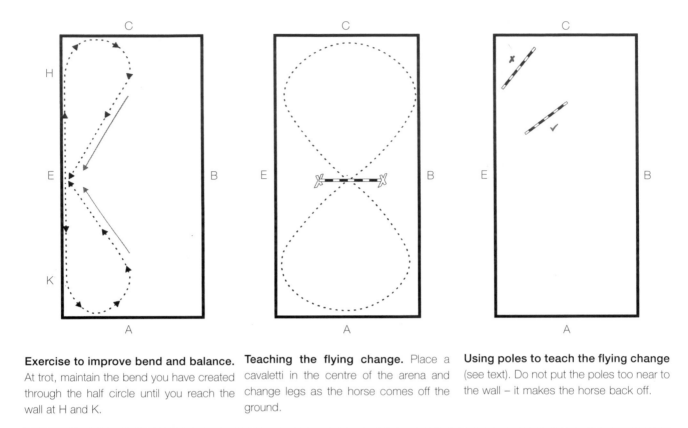

**Exercise to improve bend and balance.** At trot, maintain the bend you have created through the half circle until you reach the wall at H and K.

**Teaching the flying change.** Place a cavaletti in the centre of the arena and change legs as the horse comes off the ground.

**Using poles to teach the flying change** (see text). Do not put the poles too near to the wall – it makes the horse back off.

canter when learning to canter on a circle as part of their formative training. Some people would raise their eyebrows and say that you need to have an established, balanced canter before you attempt to teach the flying change. However, I believe that if you ask horses to do 'new tricks' when they are innocent and offering to do things for you the job becomes more of a game and less of a drama. A horse cantering loose in the school will often perform a change quite naturally, so we are only trying to transform a natural movement into something we can instigate at a given time by a given signal.

To prepare for the flying change, make sure that your horse is in balance and has enough impulsion in his hind legs to make the jump from one hind leg to the other – hind leg being the operative word because if the horse changes legs behind he will invariably change in front, but if he changes in front it does not necessarily follow that he will also change behind. To obtain the change, you should attempt physically to change your horse's bend and to push the quarters over.

For example, imagine you are on a right-hand circle

with a right-hand lead and your horse's quarters with a right-hand bend, and you want to effect a change across the diagonal of your school. As you cross the diagonal you move your horse onto a left bend, with his quarters moving to the left, and as you ask the quarters to move across and change their bend so the hind legs should automatically change their lead, following through with a change of the front legs. Effectively you have put your horse onto the left hind leg so that he is supporting himself through the left corner.

Remember your basics and what each hand and leg is meant to do – as you ask for the change your inside supporting hand becomes your outside controlling hand, and your outside controlling leg becomes the inside driving leg, but as you change the bend you must offer your horse some support with the outside rein so he does not fall onto his forehand. As you change your aids you are physically changing the bend and pushing the quarters slightly towards the inside to make him move from one hind leg to the other.

Initially, ride your horse across the diagonal, ask him

to perform a flying change and see what he offers. If he performs a change without any problem, breathe a sigh of relief and say: 'Thank goodness for that!' If he does not then you have to think about other methods of teaching him the flying change. The important thing is that you must be able to maintain a balance throughout the change. It is not a case of throwing your horse off the balance of one shoulder and then throwing him on to the other and hoping that he changes – he probably will, but he will more than likely change legs in front and not behind. That is the most common fault seen in the jumping arena.

The mistake made by some riders is that they aim their horses towards the wall when asking for a flying change. This makes the horse very defensive and he will not change legs so freely while he is backing off from the wall and throwing his weight onto the shoulder. It is not important where you ask for the change of leg: you can ask for the change of lead on the diagonal, or you can make a canter circle and ask for the change of lead as you change direction onto the opposite circle (as in a figure-of-eight), or you can change from counter canter to true canter on a straight line. It is better that you vary the point of asking for the change so that your horse learns to listen to the aids rather than looks to change automatically at a certain point.

Show jumping horses usually develop an instinct for changing legs on the corner, as they have to do it so often and you can use the horse's anticipation to help perform the exercise. Most young horses are quite willing to perform a flying change naturally and quickly learn to change to order when given the correct aids. A few horses do genuinely find it physically difficult to change legs in canter and with these horses we have to try and teach the flying change and to do that we certainly do need to have a better canter.

To teach your horse the flying change, use a small pole raised about 6 inches off the ground, or a cavaletti, in the middle of your arena at the centre of a figure-of-eight, and change legs as the horse comes off the ground. In order to do this you have to have good balance and timing. You need to keep your horse in balance all the way to the pole, and as he comes off the floor you need to change the bend and *slightly* shift your weight so that your inside leg becomes the outside leg etc. It is important to use your eye and sense of rhythm and an open rein rather than a pulling hand. Use the pole to enable your horse to get into the habit of changing legs as he changes direction. Then you can put the pole near the end of the diagonal line coming towards the corner so that as you come across the pole he changes leg onto the new lead. When you feel that your horse is responding confidently to your aids you can lower the pole, and soon take it away altogether.

# CHAPTER 8

# *Jumping Under Saddle*

Although your horse has been introduced to jumping small fences on the lunge and loose, without a rider, adding a rider to the equation changes the horse's whole equilibrium. He now has to learn to balance himself over the jump with a considerable weight on his back. By remaining in balance with your horse, as discussed in Chapter 5, 'The Rider's Position', you will help him considerably, but it is best to start your ridden jumping with the simplest of exercises and work up from there. You should begin with trotting over poles on the ground.

Using ground poles either in a straight line or on a curve will teach you and your horse to have a sense of rhythm and tempo. They will also develop your horse's strength and musculature as he has to make higher steps.

Begin by trotting through three or four poles placed either 4ft 6ins (1.35m) apart (so that your horse steps over a pole with every stride) or 9ft (2.70m) apart (so that he steps over a pole with every other stride). You can continue to add poles, up to a row of twelve, as your horse becomes stronger and more confident.

An exercise that will help you to develop a sense of rhythm is to count aloud as you trot toward, through and away from the poles. Start counting 'one-two, one-two' as your horse's front feet touch the ground, and try to establish an even, unhurried pace all the time you are trotting.

Counting aloud, whether at walk, trot or canter, is an excellent way of assessing the speed and regularity of your horse's paces. Counting will also help you on the approach to a fence, keeping you calm and dissuading you from upping the tempo on your approach, thus preventing your horse from flattening and rushing into his fences.

Raising the ground poles by 3-4ins (75–100mm) in wooden blocks will make your horse even more aware of where he is putting his feet and will further develop the muscles in his neck, shoulder, back and hindquarters. This work is quite strenuous, so do not overdo it or the muscles will become strained rather than strengthened.

When you and your horse feel confident and in balance through a row of ground poles, you can build a small, single cross-pole or put a cavaletti at the end of the row. The advantage of jumping cross-poles is that, from the very start, you are encouraging your horse to jump through the middle of his fences.

Remember to count as you move through the poles towards the jump and maintain an even tempo. In theory, your position shouldn't change over the jump, but do be prepared for your horse to make a huge leap over even the smallest fence and, if necessary hold on to the neck strap of the martingale or his mane – anything to prevent you from being left behind your horse's action, catching at his mouth, and/or landing heavily on his neck or loins, which will make him uncomfortable and less willing to try the whole thing again.

By increasing the distance between the ground poles

**Trot poles on the ground.** Moving nicely through a line of trotting poles. Note the horse's elevation and general 'springability'.

**Raised trot poles.** Moving on to tackle raised trotting poles, either at 4ft 6ins (1.35m) or at 9ft (2.70m) apart.

to 10–12ft (3.05–3.65m) you can begin cantering towards the fence; continue to count – and relax! Keep your body supple and your arms soft and elastic.

Gradually remove the ground poles and introduce your horse to a variety of small fences – uprights, oxers and triple bars. A single pole placed 1ft (30cm) in front of the fence, known as a ground line, will encourage your horse to lower his head, look at the fence and take off in the correct place. Use the points below to make sure that you are building safe fences, and bear in mind how your horse's vision operates (see page 51) as this has a considerable bearing on his jumping and your fence building.

## Fencing materials

Practice fences do not have to be immaculate or even brightly painted, but they do have to be safe. Wooden wings and poles should not be full of splinters or nails – for your sake as well as your horse's. Rustic, machine-planed poles can be bought fairly cheaply from farm shops or timber merchants. You can then either paint them yourself or buy plastic pole-rolls to brighten them up. However, pole-rolls may prove a false economy as they may not last as long as a good lick of paint, and they can flap disconcertingly on a breezy day.

Make sure that your jump wings will stand up to

**The first jump.** A simple cross-pole, approached from a raised trotting pole 9ft (2.7m) away, is a good introduction to jumping.

**An easy oxer.** This youngster is tackling his first oxer. Note how the fence is small and inviting. Don't be too ambitious at this stage. Keep the jumps simple and easy, to build confidence.

**Jumping fillers.** These two pictures show a young horse clearly impressed with the fillers and going higher, not 'freezing' or panicking. A good start.

being moved from place to place, and that they are light enough for you or your helper to carry.

Plastic jump wings are an excellent alternative to wood. They are durable and, usually, light and easy to move around. However, be very careful when you buy plastic poles. Most are not as heavy as wooden poles, and horses soon discover how light they are and quickly learn to treat them with contempt. Free-standing or hanging plastic fillers are fine, though, as they are heavier and tend to be used with a pole above them. Oil drums make acceptable fillers but check that they are not badly corroded and cannot roll about.

## Rules of fence construction

• Measure the height of fences from the ground to the top of the highest rail.
• Measure the width of fences from the centre of the front rail to the centre of the back rail.
• When building combinations of fences, measure the distance between them from the centre of the back rail of the first fence to the centre of the front rail of the next.
• The average stride length of a 15.2–16.2hh horse is 12ft (3.65m). Measure the distance between fences in groups of four 3ft (90cm) paces. Each group of four is equal to one of your horse's non-jumping strides. Remember to allow two paces for your horse's landing, and two for his take-off. Therefore, the measurement from the back rail of the first jump to the front

rail of the second should be eight paces (approximately 24ft/7.20m).
• When measuring distances for ponies, reduce your own stride length by 3ins (75mm) per hand. So, to provide a 12.2hh pony with one non-jumping stride between fences, the distance should be between 17ft (5.20m) and 20ft (6.10m). Aternatively, using 'adult' 3ft (90cm) strides, seven paces will give a 14.2hh pony one non-jumping stride, and six paces will give a 12.2hh pony one non-jumping stride.
• When building fences lower than 3ft (90cm) high, shorten the distances by 3ft (90cm) per horse's stride.
• When measuring distances take into account ground conditions, the terrain and the siting of fences in relation to 'home'. Allow an extra foot (30cm) per horse's stride if the fences are built on a gentle downhill slope, if your horse is travelling towards home, or if the turf is particularly springy. Reduce the distances by a foot (30cm) per horse's stride if the fences are built on an uphill slope, are sited away from home, or the going is heavy.
• When building combinations for the novice horse make the first element an encouraging fence, such as an ascending oxer, and the second element a forgiving fence, such as an upright or another ascending oxer.
• Ground-line poles encourage your horse to lower his head and neck on the approach to the fence. Always place the ground-line pole in front of the fence – never behind it. In the same vein, never put a filler behind the front rail. The exception to this rule is

when jumping a fence in both directions – as in a figure of eight – you can put a ground line either side of the fence.

- Canter poles help your horse to arrive in the correct place to jump the fence. They can be used in combinations, and in groups of fences with related distances. They should always be measured 9ft (2.75m) (i.e. three paces) back from the fence to be jumped.

- When building an oxer or a triple bar you may use a filler or have as many rails as you like on the front wings, but always have a single rail on the middle and back wings.

- Never build a triple bar in a concave shape, e.g. with the middle rail only one hole higher than the front, and the back pole four holes higher than that. This format is uninviting for the horse and will encourage him to jump flat and low.

- Always build a triple bar in a convex line, e.g. with the middle rail four holes higher than the first, and the back rail two holes higher than that.

- Empty jump cups left on fence wings are likely to injure you and your horse. Always remove jump cups that are not in use and put them somewhere safe.

- Do not ram jump wings so tightly into poles that the poles will not fall if your horse knocks them. Most likely, the wings will fall along with the poles, which

at the very least will frighten your horse and quite probably cause injury as well.

- Cross-poles will encourage your horse to jump through the middle of the fence. They are particularly useful if your horses tends to drift towards the wings when approaching a jump.

- Descending oxers are not allowed in competition but set up in training they can encourage your horse to use his shoulders powerfully and tuck up his front legs.

- A mass of brightly coloured rails or fillers will encourage bolder horses to back off, but they may frighten more timid horses.

- Always have a helper on the ground whenever you are practising at home. He or she can rebuild the fences and is on hand in the event of an emergency.

- Never be tempted to build fences that are beyond your capabilities or those of your horse.

- If you are unsure about what you are doing, don't do it!

## How your horse sees his fences

When working with your horse over fences and setting up jumps it is helpful to have some understanding of the horse's vision. Your horse's eyes are positioned in his skull so that he can see virtually all the way around his body. Each eye works independently and has a (monoc-

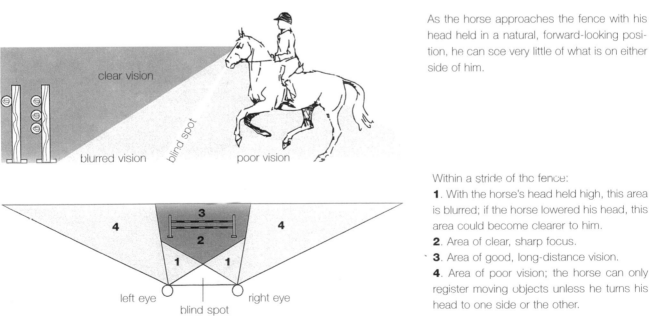

As the horse approaches the fence with his head held in a natural, forward-looking position, he can see very little of what is on either side of him.

Within a stride of the fence:
1. With the horse's head held high, this area is blurred; if the horse lowered his head, this area could become clearer to him.
2. Area of clear, sharp focus.
3. Area of good, long-distance vision.
4. Area of poor vision; the horse can only register moving objects unless he turns his head to one side or the other.

*Points to ponder…*

• *There is no such thing as great talent without great will power.*

**Peter Charles**

"Build a partnership in which you and your horse have confidence in each other. Never ask your horse to do something that you are not confident about or that you feel will frighten him."

ular) field of vision of almost 180°, but there is an area of overlap directly in front of the horse, in which the horse can focus both eyes and see things as we do, in binocular vision (see illustration on page 51). The horse's eyes are designed to help him be aware of dangers and predators; they were not positioned for the express purpose of jumping brightly coloured poles. For one thing he has a blind spot directly in front of and below his nose. This means that he loses sight of the fence once he has taken off. Therefore, his judgement of how high he has to jump to clear the fence has to be made on the approach to the fence. It also means that he has to trust his rider, knowing that it is safe to jump.

The structure of the horse's eye has two major differences from our own. Our lenses alter their shape to focus on objects as they move toward or away from us – the horse's lenses are rigid. Latest research has detected the second major difference - a strip of high-cell density known as the visual streak. Within the visual streak, which is very wide from side to side but very narrow from top to bottom, the horse's vision is extremely good, but outside of it his ability to see things sharply is poor. As a horse moves towards an object he has to raise his head to keep that object within the visual streak. Relate this to show jumping and it is now easy to appreciate **why it is very important that the rider does not try to keep the horse's head down on the approach to a jump**.

Another point for the rider to bear in mind is that as far as the horse is concerned **all** the fences in his field of vision, which is so much wider than ours, will seem equally bold and in focus. Thus it is vital that the rider guides his horse firmly towards the correct fence during a competition.

A further effect of the equine eye structure is that the closer the horse gets to an object, such as a fence, the less of that object remains in focus. So, by the time the horse is a couple of strides away from the fence only the top few inches remain sharply in focus. And once he is virtually upon the fence, it enters his blind spot and he can no longer see it – he is jumping on trust and experience.

It is believed that horses are less able than we are to judge the width (depth) of a fence. They are more likely to gauge the width of an obstacle by its general appearance; therefore if a fence looks substantial and seems to have a lot of poles, the horse is likely to think it is wide (deep). This would explain why horses often knock down poles on flimsy-looking spread fences.

It is also thought that horses are colour blind and can only see in 'black and white' – or various shades of grey. This is why the colours of poles used to build jumps can be important. The contrast between black and white poles is much greater than that between, say, yellow and white poles. If you were to mix yellow and white poles with black and white poles when building a fence, the horse's eye would automatically be drawn to the black and white poles and he would be less likely to notice the yellow and white ones.

You should also take the background into account when building fences – solidly coloured poles are more difficult to jump than banded poles as they are more likely to merge into the background. Plain green poles in a field, or rustic poles in a sand school, are likely to be very difficult for your horse to see.

# CHAPTER 9

# Seeing a Stride

The question that I am most frequently asked is: 'What is "seeing a stride"?' My answer is: 'The gift of always knowing exactly at which spot the horse will take off, and having the fundamental ability to alter the horse's approach to enable the horse to arrive at that correct take-off point.'

Riders tend to overlook the fact that horses are not blind and that they are not stupid. They have an in-built facility for survival and a very long memory. In his natural state, without a rider on his back to alter his balance and rhythm, a horse will instinctively set himself up for a fence and take off at the correct place time and time again. If a good rider gets onto the horse and rides him in rhythm and balance and at the correct speed to a fence, enabling the horse to take off from the correct spot every single time, it will not be very long before the horse begins to aim for it himself, provided, of course, that he is not interfered with.

Remember, too, that the horse's ability to judge distances is a great deal more accurate than our own and that his innate instinct is much sharper than ours, so his brain is actually working more quickly in an instinctive way than is the rider's. The horse is a prey animal and his instinct, when faced with danger, is to flee; so when the horse gets into a situation that he finds difficult or threatening, such as an incorrect or panicked approach to a jump, he will instinctively panic. This is likely to produce the result we all fear – the horse will come to an abrupt halt in front of the fence, which is a prelude to turning around and running away. Occasionally he will blindly crash straight through the jump. Alternatively he may jump too high in an attempt to protect himself, but doing so will frighten him and he will be more inclined to stop next time.

Once we have accepted that the horse is neither blind nor stupid and can, by himself, jump correctly, we are ready to add ourselves to the equation. Problems start to occur when riders are not consistent. Some riders will approach the same fence twenty times and never take off from the same spot twice. This is when the horse starts to become confused; and the more confused he becomes the more his confidence ebbs away, leading to a rapid decline in the horse's desire to jump. Firstly, he becomes a little stressed because he does not know where he is going to be asked to take off from; then he becomes tense; the tension and stress lead to further confusion, at which point he starts to hesitate – and the more he hesitates the more mistakes he makes. A downward spiral quickly ensues, usually ending up with a horse that refuses to jump at all.

The mistake that has been made by so many coaches in the past is that they have tried to standardise the correct take-off point by giving a set formula, such as: 'The take-off point for a 4-foot fence is exactly 4-foot away from the fence.' Fortunately no two horses are alike and what may be the correct take-off point for one may be way off the mark for another. If your horse is slow to fold up his front legs but is careful behind, his ideal take-off point is going to be further away from the fence than for a horse who is quick in front but lazy with his hind legs.

The fundamental rule to remember when you are riding to a fence is this:

**You must maintain the correct SPEED or TEMPO to jump the particular fence you are coming to in BALANCE and RHYTHM.**

It is a rule that comes up again and again throughout this book because it is the one important factor that remains constant. There are just a few very gifted riders who have the innate ability to judge distances, so for the majority it is a case of training, and more training, to keep the stride constant and not to keep changing the tempo.

The terrain is also very important. If you are jumping downhill your horse will naturally come to his fence on a slightly longer, flatter stride, unless you keep him collected between your legs and your hands and, again, keep the stride constant. Because he is more able to cover the ground when jumping downhill, the point at which you want your horse to take off needs to be slightly further away than if you are on the flat, so the ability to keep in balance is even more important.

When jumping uphill it is important to keep up the strength and impulsion of the canter so that your horse does not run out of steam before he reaches the jump. The take-off point when jumping uphill should be closer to the fence than when jumping on the flat so it will be necessary to maintain a more powerful, shorter stride.

Heavy going underfoot also influences where the horse takes off – heavy going can add 6 inches to the total height of the fence. Your horse needs to take off nearer to the fence to enable him to pull out of the mud, but he needs to have enough power and, probably, marginally more speed to stay within his comfort zone.

From more advanced riders the question I am most frequently asked is: 'How can I improve my ability to see a stride?' The short answer is: 'It's not easy!' (And it is not even that important!) Every coach in the world has tried a hundred different ways to explain 'how to see a stride' but no one has yet come up with a magic formula. Perhaps, rather cynically, my favourite reply to the question is: 'Everyone can see a stride ... but often it's a bad one.'

Now that you have learnt that the correct take-off point is influenced by many different factors you can begin to learn to see where your horse needs to take off from – to 'see' your horse's stride.

The first thing you have to decide when approaching the fence is the speed or tempo at which you are to travel. In deciding the speed of the approach it is necessary to include the horse's nature in the equation. To ask a naturally fast and fizzy horse to go slowly is likely to make him pent up and upset; he will learn to go against the rider, begin to hollow and may ultimately become uncontrollable. You have to allow him to move forward – but under control. Having found the tempo at which the horse is happy to be ridden, you then have to discipline yourself to maintain that tempo and to ride the horse at his fences at that tempo. It is important to maintain that same speed and rhythm throughout the approach. You also have to understand that you may

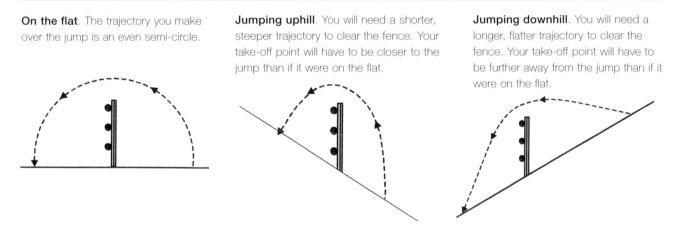

**On the flat**. The trajectory you make over the jump is an even semi-circle.

**Jumping uphill**. You will need a shorter, steeper trajectory to clear the fence. Your take-off point will have to be closer to the jump than if it were on the flat.

**Jumping downhill**. You will need a longer, flatter trajectory to clear the fence. Your take-off point will have to be further away from the jump than if it were on the flat.

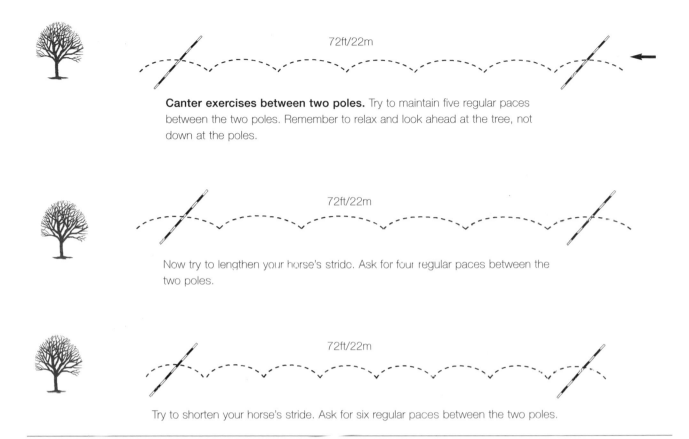

**Canter exercises between two poles.** Try to maintain five regular paces between the two poles. Remember to relax and look ahead at the tree, not down at the poles.

72ft/22m

Now try to lengthen your horse's stride. Ask for four regular paces between the two poles.

72ft/22m

Try to shorten your horse's stride. Ask for six regular paces between the two poles.

have to alter the tempo for the approach to different jumps. A narrow stile will require a slower, more cautious approach than, say, a big wide oxer, which will need a bolder approach.

At the beginning you have to convince yourself that the jump is the least important part of the equation – it is the stride pattern, the tempo, which is all-important. I tell my riders to forget about the fence altogether, so that they concentrate entirely on a rhythmic canter, and on the maintenance of the tempo. The horse can then get on with focusing his attention forward, rather than thinking backwards about what his rider is about to do or not do in order to make a mess of jumping the approaching fence.

If the horse is worried about what you, sitting on his back, are going to do next he is not going to be concentrating on the fence in front of him. However, if you can ignore the pole and just set up the stride pattern then he is not going to be thinking about you but about the fence ahead. It is incredibly difficult not to think about the approaching jump so it is really

important that you keep the jumps very small until you feel totally confident riding to the fence without worrying about whether or not you can see a stride.

The greatest tool for improving your judgement of distance is a balanced, rhythmic canter that has controlled impulsion. Without a good canter it is impossible to achieve a good jump. Exercises to improve the canter are mentioned elsewhere, but a good exercise to help you to start improving your ability to keep a good canter on the approach to, and in between, fences is to put two poles on the ground approximately five non-jumping strides apart (about 72ft/22m). Set up your canter in another part of the school and attain a good rhythm and correct tempo. Come off the corner and canter towards the poles with the sole purpose of maintaining the rhythm and tempo. Focus on a point beyond the poles (say, a tree) and do not be tempted to look down at the poles as you cross them. (See illustrations above.)

Do not worry if your horse leaps the poles wildly or gets six, or even seven, strides between them, just

4

3

**Using canter poles on the approach to a jump.** Canter poles help the horse to have a rhythmic, balanced approach to each jump. Each pole is 10ft (3m) apart for an approximately 16hh horse. As a very rough guide you can reduce this distance by 9ins (23cm) for each hand smaller. I reiterate: this is a rough guide only – your coach should know your horse's stride and adjust the poles to suit.

continue on your circle trying to keep the rhythm. Once your horse is cantering evenly through the poles on five strides try to decrease the tempo so that he gets six or seven strides in between the two. Although you are trying to shorten your horse's stride, try to maintain impulsion in the canter, but remember – don't look down at the poles. You are trying to develop a feel for the correct canter and looking down will shift your focus. Now increase the tempo so that he gets just four strides between the poles, but do not let the canter become flat. Then vary the number of strides from four to six.

Whether lengthening or shortening the stride, keep the horse in balance throughout the exercise. Remember, lengthening does not mean flattening or galloping; likewise shortening does not mean reducing the power in your horse's stride.

Once you feel totally confident carrying out this exercise without looking at the poles, you are ready to raise the poles a little, but be sensible – the main object of the exercise is to increase your confidence, not the size of the jump. By learning to alter your horse's canter

stride you are increasing your chances of being able to reach the fence at the correct take-off point and you are giving yourself a greater range of options. If you repeat the exercise enough times, you will start to pick up from a long way back not only how many strides in terms of numbers it will take to arrive at the fence, but also whether or not the rhythm and tempo you have will bring you to the fence at the correct take-off point.

Another good exercise to help you develop your feel and judgement is to lay down seven or eight poles 10 feet (3.05 metres) apart and to canter over them. Again, don't look at the poles, just maintain your horse's rhythm. Eventually, this will become instinctive and therefore easier. Your horse should be able to canter through this grid without altering his stride in any way; he maintains the same tempo all the way through. When you are confident over poles you can put a small jump at the end of them, 10 feet (3.05 metres) away from the poles (see photos above). This will teach you that it is possible to maintain a good canter at least seven or eight strides away from the fence and eventually, on the whole approach from your initial turn.

Once you have developed the skill of being able to approach a fence without the need to look at it, by feeling the horse's stride working correctly underneath you, you will eventually begin to feel more confident. You will be able to concentrate more and more on keeping your horse at the correct speed and be satisfied that you are riding in balance. You will begin to know instinctively whether a certain point is a good or bad

place to take off from. If that point is a bad one then you will have to make an adjustment. The adjustment that you make is crucial. You have two choices – to lengthen the stride or to shorten it – but you have just one opportunity to get it right. That one chance comes at the precise moment when you realise that you are not going to meet the fence at the correct point. If you do not make that one instantaneous correction, you will probably start to panic and will either pull or push until you make a mess of things; either way, your horse will lose balance and confidence.

The more you continue to ride at fences without worrying about them, the greater the distance will become from which you can be confident of arriving at the fence in good form to jump it well. Top-class riders are able to tell from ten or twelve strides away from the fence whether or not they are going to take off from the correct point for their horse. The very best will do this entirely naturally; however, many top riders are just very well trained and they have attained the skill of judgement through practice. You cannot expect or hope to be as good as the very best but hard work will help you to achieve a sense of balance, rhythm, tempo and judgement, which you can continue to improve on throughout your show jumping career.

# CHAPTER 10

# Getting from Fence to Fence

How does riding a horse that is in balance feel? Wonderful! He comes to the fence with his weight in the hind leg, carrying himself forward with impulsion and at the correct speed. He jumps and lands in balance, not running away from you but just continuing at a correct and even pace. This is the situation you are striving to create.

How does riding a horse that is out of balance feel? Terrible! He will generally pull down onto his forehand, fall in on his inside shoulder or drift out towards his outside shoulder. There is nothing quite so uncomfortable as trying to ride a horse to a fence when he is pulling down, dragging you out of the saddle and out of balance. A situation develops where there is no balance at all between you and your horse, leading to a state of nil co-ordination and nil co-operation. Your horse will run to his fences with his weight on his forehand and then has to try and lift up his shoulders to jump the fence whilst the rest of his weight is trying to push his shoulders down.

Each time a horse jumps a fence he initiates a great deal of power – he travels through the air at a considerable velocity, and if you have no control over that power, any problem you have will quickly magnify. Riding around a set of show jumps in an unbalanced state is accumulative. Each time your horse jumps **in** to a fence out of balance he will land out of it **more** out of balance. There is a fine line between being in and out of balance, between having rhythm and lacking rhythm,

and being in or out of control. Repetition is the key to achieving many of the qualities required to keep it all together, but unfortunately there is a tendency to replicate bad habits more easily than good habits.

In your mind's eye see a picture of your horse cantering in rhythm and balance, with yourself sitting in balance; your horse is listening, waiting and responding to each aid; see your horse jumping the first fence and landing without rushing off; watch him taking three or four strides to the next fence without increasing or decreasing his speed, and see him jumping the next fence in exactly the same manner. This is the picture you are now going to create as a reality. From now on you should always visualise yourself doing things well (positive visualisation) – and never imagining doing things wrongly, otherwise you will draw yourself into doing them wrongly (negative visualisation).

The first point to make about the approach to the fence is that in the show jumping arena your approach to any fence is likely to come off a corner or immediately after another jump. You can teach your horse to jump at home in a straight line until you are blue in the face but he will not be any better equipped to compete. So when schooling at home you should approach fences off circles and corners and from related distances in both straight and curved lines.

The penultimate corner before the jump is the last moment in which you can make major adjustments. If they are not made then, you have left it rather too late!

**Turning between fences.** Being able to approach and leave a fence off a balanced curve is at the heart of successful show jumping. Here the rider has prepared his turn whilst in the air (1–2). His horse has landed on the correct leg, easing his passage around the corner (3). The turn progresses smoothly, and horse and rider jump the next fence effortlessly (4).

The adjustments you should think about making include putting your horse in balance, and ensuring that as he turns the corner he is full square over his inside hind leg, pushing himself around the corner and not leaning heavily into your hand.

You can make the half-halt aid or slow down before the corner, or you can encourage more forward movement in the corner. Whatever the adjustment, it must ensure that your horse comes out of the penultimate corner with the right amount of activity, balance, rhythm and tempo. It is always your job to ensure that your horse is in balance. This requires speed, skill and a forward-thinking rider who has a good instinct for balance, a good, firm position and a sound use of leg and hand.

Once you have put your horse in balance through the corners and have straightened him up from the final corner to the fence you are approaching, there should be no more corrections to make. The problem with riding a **bad** corner is that it will lead to a bad approach. If your horse comes to a fence off a corner out of balance and too much on his forehand, his weight will be thrown onto the outside shoulder. He will jump the fence at too sharp an angle and will drift outwards across the fence. Once you have a bad approach all you can do is hold your horse together between hand and leg and rely on his good will and natural ability to get you over the fence. If your horse is drifting badly across the fence, he will need to have even more natural ability, as the obstacle he is jumping will be wider than the coursebuilder intended (see diagram below).

Psychologically, the approach to the next fence begins when you are actually in the air over the fence you are jumping. Physically, the approach starts as the horse puts his first foot on the ground during landing. You should be thinking in the air about the type of approach and jump you have just achieved. If your approach was a good, balanced one and the jump feels right, with your horse in a good, round bascule, then your landing is likely to be balanced, as is your move away from the fence and the approach to the next. If your horse has powered into the fence, jumped in a flat trajectory over it and is likely to land running on his forehand, then you will need to bring him back into balance before the next fence.

It can even be useful to try and practise coming into a jump a little too fast, thus creating a situation in which the horse is going to land flat, so that you can learn to round him up on the landing stride and create the powerful, balanced canter you need to jump the next fence in good style. You must shorten the stride with the leg and the hand – it is no good just pulling on the reins, because that will just make your horse hollow. You must use your reins and your legs to initiate a bigger, rounder canter stride and you must practise this at home.

**Jumping straight and at an angle**. At the beginning of your horse's training he should be encouraged to jump straight across his fences. If he jumps crookedly he has further to travel across the fence, because it effectively becomes wider. Later on in his career, when he needs to win in jump-off situations, he will have to learn to jump across fences at an angle.

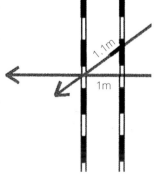

Certainly, things can go wrong on the approach to a fence, and if this happens you may need to adapt a 'seat of the pants' style of riding so your instinctive skills kick in. But a rider who habitually turns corners badly should not be in the competition arena; he should go back to square one, sorting out his horse's balance on the flat before entering the arena again.

The final approach to the fence begins at the last corner before it, and it is from here that you have to develop the appropriate pace and impulsion for the fence or fences. The balance of your horse depends largely on what pace you are travelling at, and the height and width of the fence you are jumping govern that pace. You need to adapt the canter to suit the fence you are approaching. If you are jumping a vertical fence you may need to approach it a little more slowly, but if you are jumping a great big, wide triple bar you are not going to want to take it from walk!

You must ride according to what you think the horse's reaction to the fence is going to be when you reach it. A big, wide fence is likely to make your horse back off, whereas a straight vertical will not, so **you** have to do a certain amount of the backing off. You will need to contain your horse in the hand more when coming to a vertical than you will coming to an oxer, where you are travelling in a more forward manner so that your horse meets it with a forward-thinking stride and is able to make the ground to clear all the parts of the fence.

The ideal situation is that your horse lands over every fence in a steady rhythm, carrying himself without effort, and that he does not slow down or speed up without being asked to do so – in short he allows you to ride him. Corrections and improvements are progressive – you will not make everything happen all at the same time. You will have set-backs, so it is important not to get too hung up about it. Miracles never happen – horses have to learn, and learn gradually.

Try to think on two levels – with a plan, and instinctively. When you set up an exercise or walk a show jumping course (see page 94) you should have a plan as to how you are going to approach each fence. The first time your horse has ever seen these fences is when you are asking him to jump them, so make sure that you have worked out how you are going to ask him to jump them. You must make a clear and determined effort to walk the course properly so that you can plan precisely what you are going to do. Once you have made your plan, you must stick to it – as far as is possible! General Patton said, 'A good plan executed half well is better than no plan at all.'

There is a saying: 'Plans do not always work, but if you do not have one, it can never work.' My version of this is: 'If you make a plan things **may** go wrong, if you do not have a plan things **will** go wrong.'

Study the course, walk the course, think about it and ride it in your mind before you ride it on your horse. Think about all the things that **might** go wrong, how you will prevent things from going wrong and how you are going to react if they **do** go wrong. This may sound like a complicated procedure to go through to jump a few poles, but it is important to remember that if you have a plan you will feel a lot more in control of the situation and this feeling of control and confidence will be transmitted to your horse.

Thinking instinctively means that you know **what** is happening **when** it is happening and are able to react quickly and efficiently to that particular feel. If your horse lands short and is not appearing to make any ground then you might try to kick and gallop forward to the next fence – instinctive but not effective! Your horse will flatten and become unbalanced on the approach to the next fence. To be instinctive *and* effective you need to think 'balance, rhythm and tempo' all the time. So when your horse lands flat you have **instinctively** to drive him forward with your leg into a strong, restraining hand, collecting his hind legs underneath you. You need to put all his power and weight back into his quarters – where it needs to be to return to a well-balanced, round canter. You must learn to keep your hand off the 'panic button', which needs confidence and self-discipline. Confidence and discipline come with practice, repetition, training – and planning!

If an instinctive rider is planning correctly, things will work. His instinct will tell him quickly when things are going wrong. If he has quick reactions then he will have even more time in which to plan his next move – the quicker a sportsman thinks, the more time he has to react and adjust.

## Useful exercises

An exercise to improve your horse's balance on the landing stride is to use four fences in a long line, with three- to five-stride distances in between them. The fences need not be very large, indeed if they are quite small your horse may land flat and running to begin with, and that is exactly the problem this exercise is designed to solve. Start with the fences at 3ft (90cm) and raise them, as your horse progresses, up to 3ft 10ins (1.15m). (See illustration below.)

Your aim is to approach all the fences in exactly the same rhythm and tempo each time and to monitor the quality of each jump. If your horse jumps the first in a flat manner and lands heavily on his forehand the chances are that he will run in an unbalanced manner to the second. To avoid this you must be ready to bring him to a halt as soon as he has landed over the first fence.

The reason for bringing the horse to a halt is to gain his full attention and to start making him think about what he is doing. The next time you jump the line, your horse will be a little more careful about how he jumps each fence. However, the momentum of jumping three or four fences may start to make him flat again, so it is probable that you will have to stop him again after the third or fourth fence. You may have to repeat this exercise several times to focus your horse's mind on what you are doing.

Sometimes this 'pulling up' exercise is not all that pretty – it is not crucial that it is pretty – it **is** crucial

**Exercise using a line of four fences (see text above). Approach all the fences in the same tempo and rhythm**

16 yards = 3 horse strides     24 yards = 5 horse strides     20 yards = 4 horse strides

**Initiating a turn in the air.** (1) Landing onto a left-hand bend. (2) Landing onto a right-hand bend. In both of these photos the riders have looked the way they are going and have shifted their weight fractionally toward the inside of the bend. Both horses have responded by landing on the correct leg, although the horse on the left is not yet turning into the bend with his body.

that it is functional. It has absolutely no function if you allow your horse to run on past fences rather than halt in a straight line or jump the fence out of control. It is important that when you ask for the halt your horse halts, but this does not mean that you try to pull his back teeth out! The benefits of the exercise are that your horse should become attentive and be listening to every single aid that you give him. The aim of the exercise is that you should be able to return your horse to a state of balance each time he lands over a fence and that he should arrive at the next fence in balance.

Another good 'balancing act' is to practise initiating turns in the air (see photos above). This helps your horse to land on the correct lead and also helps him to establish his balance after the jump. It also gives your horse

something to think about and lessens the chances of him rushing off upon the landing stride. If you repeat an exercise a few times your horse will start to antici–pate the next move. In this exercise we use the horse's anticipation to benefit his training.

If you initiate a turn to the right whilst in the air three or four times, your horse will begin to anticipate that bend to the right and will start shifting his weight to the right mid-air, landing with his right leg leading. If, however, during your next jump you initiate a turn to the left, your horse, with his weight already loaded to the right, will land lightly on his left leg and shoulder, putting him in better balance.

The anticipation has helped you because your horse has put his weight onto the right shoulder and you have immediately taken it off that shoulder, putting him onto a left lead so he will be light in the left shoulder.

As with every jumping exercise you undertake, as you make the approach monitor your canter and consider the condition of your horse's stride. He should be going forward with impulsion, in front of the leg, and feel comfortable in the rein contact. On the last stride you must think about the moves you need to make. As your horse starts to take off you must look into the turn with your head up. Your eyes are important – make sure they are looking in the direction you intend to travel. Start the bend with an open, turning rein and increase the weight in your inside stirrup.

Do not exaggerate the leaning into the turn, or your weight on the inside will push your horse in the opposite direction. Moving your hand to an open rein position and turning your head is likely to create sufficient weight adjustment into the inside stirrup for your horse to follow. Your rein is leading your horse into the bend, not pulling him into it. If you try to pull your horse into the bend he is likely to set his jaw against you and run straight or away from the blocking hand.

In both of the exercises you should ride in the forward, balanced seat with your weight just off the saddle. This is important because you do not want your weight to influence the forward movement of your horse. What your weight **must** influence is balance. If your weight is continually rocking forward and backwards your horse's balance and attention will be disturbed by these shifts and he will not be able to hear your aids.

Practise at home every skill you think you will need. Practise turning into corners and halting, riding through corners, turning out of corners, swinging corners, riding through corners without changing the rhythm or tempo, making short turns that you are going to need in a jump off, half-halts, halting from canter and cantering from halt – everything! Without practice at home you will not be able to perform in the arena.

# CHAPTER 11

# Related Distances

We say that fences are connected by a related distance when two or more fences are close enough together that the way you jump the first is going to directly affect the way you are able to jump the following fence(s). A related distance can be as short as one stride from the next fence, or as far away as six or seven, or even ten strides, according to some schools of thought. Most people consider any fences placed between one and five strides apart to be related. They can be placed in a straight line or on a curved line, which are commonly called a 'dog leg'. I prefer to use the term curved line, as the curve may be shallow or sharp and can be described as necessary.

There are several things that may influence how a related distance is jumped. The two most important words to remember are balance and tempo. If you are out of balance and riding too fast as you approach and jump the first part of a related distance you will land running, on the forehand and further out of balance as you approach and jump the second part. If you approach the fences too slowly and your horse makes too steep an arc over the first part, he will land too short for the second part. This means that you will feel you have to start kicking and driving to reach the second part and then you are back in the first scenario, approaching the second part too fast and out of balance.

What decides the speed at which you are going to approach the first part of the related distance is the format of the related distance. Is it a vertical to an oxer, an oxer to a vertical, a vertical to a double or an oxer to a double, or is it a treble combination? All of these things are thought out when you walk the course and pace the distances between fences. You study and you make a plan. The correct tempo depends entirely on the fences and the distances between them. If the distance is too long then you will have to approach the first part a little bit quicker than if the distance seemed 'spot on' or too short. That way you will land moving forward just a fraction, making the distance suitable for your horse to take off for the second part in balance. If the distance seems far too long then it will be necessary for you to make the horse add an extra stride to arrive at the second part in balance.

Adding a stride between two fences is a very skilful thing because it requires that you use your hands **and** your legs to influence the length of the horse's stride, the take-off stride and the way the horse jumps. When you use your hands and legs to make the stride shorter, you are effecting a very subtle half-halt. However, the difference between the half-halt that we talked about when working the horse on the flat and this half-halt is that now, once you have achieved the shortened stride asked for by the half-halt, you are going to maintain it all the way to the next fence, so that each stride will be in balance and more active.

What you do not want to do is to allow your horse to run faster to the fence and then suddenly panic and make an adjustment in front of the fence. This will make the last stride weak and hesitant, whereas what we really want is for that last stride to be perfect. If you allow your horse to run to the fence, making an adjustment in the last stride, one of several things will happen:

- he will crash straight through the fence,
- he will stop,
- he will jump in an inverted style, taking poles with him, or
- he will duck out at the last instant.

Always, in show jumping, you are striving to make the take-off stride perfect, so the ingredients for that stride – the balance, the impulsion, the speed and the rhythm all have to be blended precisely to achieve a correct result. If all the strides are exactly the same length when approaching the fence then your horse will be able to take off in balance.

Many riders will have a problem with adjusting their horse's stride because horses learn to run forward, especially if they have been kicked forward initially. The show jumping rider has to be able to lengthen and shorten the horse's stride almost instantaneously because, as you have already learned, the show jumper must have an infinitely adjustable stride. Often in event riding, during the cross-country phase, the most important thing the horse has to be able to do is to **lengthen** his stride, not shorten it. Event riders tend to put all their eggs in one basket and ride forward in the hope that the horse, because of the way he is taught across country to go forward, will be able to deal with everything in that manner. Unfortunately show jumps knock

**Tim Stockdale**

66 Riders should try and produce as much rhythm in their work as possible. If you can maintain a good rhythm when you are cantering and jumping a course then everything will seem a lot sweeter. If you are continually increasing and decreasing your tempo, and if your transitions are jerky and harsh, then ultimately your job will be a lot harder.

Be aware of what your horse is doing underneath you. Once you begin to concentrate on your rhythm you will become aware of his stride pattern and of what his legs are doing. As a result of this you will begin to feel that your horse's legs are an extension of you and that is the whole purpose of riding – that the horse and his rider are as one. 99

down, so one of the most important lessons that event riders have to learn is that they **can** adjust strides to be shorter as well as longer.

This is a very tough problem to solve and the solu-

**The mathematics of related distances**

| 16 yards = 3 horse strides | 24 yards = 5 horse strides | 20 yards = 4 horse strides |
|---|---|---|
| 16 yards = 16 of your paces = 2 yards for your horse's landing + 3 x 4 yards for 3 non-jumping strides + 2 yards for your horse's take-off | 24 yards = 24 of your paces – 2 yards for your horse's landing + 5 x 4 yards for 5 non-jumping strides + 2 yards for your horse's take-off | 20 yards = 20 of your paces = 2 yards for your horse's landing + 4 x 4 yards for 4 non-jumping strides + 2 yards for your horse's take-off |

(1 yard = 0.91m)

tions may seem, at first, to need rather a tough attitude. If your horse jumps the first fence in a related distance and then runs blindly forward, you must pull up to a halt, as described in Chapter 10. Your horse must be taught that he is not allowed to run on unthinkingly and that he must listen and pay attention to you at all times. You may have to do this two or three times before your horse gets the message. The first couple of times may not be a very pretty sight – he may throw his head up or down, cross his jaw or swing his quarters, but he **must** pay attention when he lands over that first part of the related distance.

With a young horse it is desirable to teach him all the skills mentioned above – i.e. to shorten or lengthen his stride between two fences, whilst always remaining in balance. If you and your horse are in harmony and balance when you land over the first part of a related distance, then ninety-nine per cent of the time you will clear the second part, so try to occupy your mind with two thoughts when training:

- firstly, planning; and
- secondly, reacting instinctively.

---

**Planning your route.** There is more than one route through a curved line, but fences in a straight line do not give you 'options'.

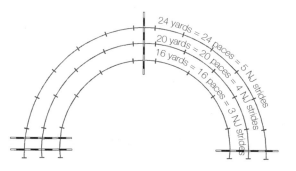

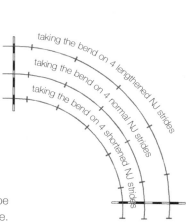

If you 'walk' every possible line between curved related distances you will be ready to take alternative routes to your intended path should the need arise.

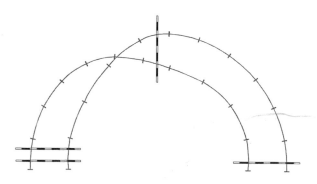

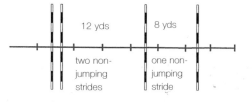

Here the horse moves from the outside wing of the middle fence to the inside wing of the final element, or vice versa. Thus he may take 5 non-jumping strides between the first two elements and 3 non-jumping strides between the final two elements, or vice versa.

Straight line = no options.

In the 'planning mode' everything is orderly, everything is organised in your head, you know what you are going to do and how you are going to react to everything according to your plan. You must think to yourself as you land over the fence that it is very important to do what you intended to do.

If it is possible to carry out your plan then it will invariably work, but if your plans have gone awry then it is very important to think very quickly and instinctively. You must act on instinct and you must make that instinct work for you. So if you have **planned** to take five strides to the next fence but your horse has landed a little steep and is running, you must react **instinctively**. You must instinctively know what is happening, instinctively know when things are going wrong and instinctively know precisely what you need to do to put things right again. Your instinct should have started to take over almost before your horse took off, because you will have felt him lose control at that all-important last stride, and realise that he is going to land out of balance. You need to start thinking and reacting instinctively while your horse is still in the air so that you are mentally and physically ready to act as soon as he lands.

To be able to plan, and think instinctively, takes time and practice, and you must learn to speed up your brain. How do you do that? Well, you cannot enter a competition and say to yourself 'Today, I am going to think really quickly.' You must try, at home, to dream up as many scenarios as you can, and then try to think of ways in which you will cope with them.

Assume that any course in a competition arena is made up of several different exercises linked together to make a complete challenge for both horse and rider. If you practise as many of those exercises as you can at home, you are not going to be taken by surprise when you get into the arena. The way to practise related distances is not to start off with setting up huge oxers at difficult distances. Instead you should put up very small fences and vary the distances between them.

I usually start off by putting just a pole on the floor and measuring the distance between it and another pole placed either on a straight line or a curved line. Stride out (measure) the distance in multiples of four times your normal paces (strides), which should be approximately 3ft (90cm) long; each of your four-pace groups equating to one horse stride. Try to educate (standard-

ise) your paces to the desired 3ft/90cm – as you will rarely have a tape measure with you, you should begin to learn to pace evenly and to know, with a fair degree of accuracy, the length of your paces. It is no good striding out in multiples of four of your normal paces if your normal paces are only 2ft (60cm) long or 3ft 6ins (1.05m) long as the whole project will be thrown into disarray and your horse will become a very confused chap!

Educate yourself in any way you see fit. You can cut a length of wood to 3ft (90cm) long and teach yourself that from the back of one heel to the front of your other toe as you take a stride is exactly 3ft (90cm) long, or you can mark a path at 3ft intervals so that you can get into a 3ft rhythm. Whichever way you choose, the end result will be that you can walk every distance on every course in exactly the same way. The uniformity of walking that distance will help you when you come to walking entire courses.

Now, back to our poles. This exercise is similar to those shown on page 55 but it does have some subtle differences. Ensure that the poles are easily approached and that the going underfoot is good. Lay out two poles on the ground on a curve, with four, five or six strides in between them. As you canter your horse through the two poles see how many strides your horse takes to cover the ground between them in his normal stride pattern. When cantering through a curved line it is important that you canter straight through the **middle** of the curve, aiming for the centre of the pole, riding the curve as you have **planned** (see drawing on facing page).

Later on, you can practise taking a short or long line to alter the distance between the poles, but not yet! When jumping related distances on a curve it is vital that you have walked the distance and assessed how you are going to ride the arc – you cannot leave it to luck. Walk the distance, look back and see where you have come from, and look forward and see where you are going, so that you can decide where the curve is going to start and end. The most important thing to remember when riding a curved line is that as soon as you are in the air, jumping the first fence, your eye should be locked on to the second.

Another way that you can teach yourself to ride correctly through a related distance is to make a passage through the curve using two poles and a cone (the layout shown in the top diagram on page 101 is similar). This gives you an opportunity to find a true line.

If you have set up a five-stride distance and your horse has bowled along and covered the ground between them in three strides, you know that you are going to be in deep trouble when you start to jump fences. Alternatively, if he puts in six or seven very short strides you know that you are going to have to make some adjustments as the obstacles become bigger and wider. However, it must be stressed that a shorter stride is infinitely more desirable than a long, flat stride.

If your horse comes into the first category, having a long, raking stride, you will have to put together an exercise to shorten his stride. You need to gain his attention after the first pole. Canter him over the first pole and bring him to a halt about three or four strides later. Bring him around again and this time ask him to halt within two or three strides of the first pole. Your aim, through this exercise, is to make your horse pay attention to the aids so that he does not go blindly on whether the poles are there or not. Once you have his attention you can almost disregard the poles and

**Canter poles.** Canter poles can be used to encourage your horse to lengthen or shorten his stride, depending on the distance between them.

concentrate on shortening your horse's stride. Get as many strides in between the two poles as you can. As his canter becomes rounder, shorter and more engaged then the adjustment between the two poles will become easier.

Even then, your large-striding horse may still prefer to stand off his fences and to jump them with a big, bold jump rather than to get in close and make an athletic jump. However, he must learn to come in deep to his fences otherwise he will be in trouble as the fences increase in size. These simple exercises help to build a base of confidence and knowledge for you and your horse. If you know that you can adjust and shorten your horse's stride at home you will have the confidence to do so in the arena, and as your horse becomes accustomed to you asking him to do different things with his stride he will not panic when you ask for a quick shortening during a competition. Exercises using poles on the ground, teaching your horse to vary his length of stride, will be very influential as the jumps get higher and wider.

If your horse fits into the latter category, that of a horse with a short stride, you do not want to alter him a great deal. He probably has a naturally springy stride, which is desirable for show jumping, but if we assume that your horse has sufficient talent and you have sufficient talent, enthusiasm and ambition to go on in the show jumping world then you need to be sure that he too is infinitely adjustable. Canter poles are of particular benefit to the horse with a short stride, although they can be used with good effect for any horse, teaching it to have a regular, even stride.

This time we try to take a stride **out** when cantering between two obstacles. Once you have landed you **could** flap the reins and kick to lengthen your horse's stride, but although you **may** increase the length of his stride you are more likely to turn him into a nervous wreck or, at the least, turn his nice, bouncy stride into a flat, hurried one. What you **really** need to do to lengthen his stride is to use lots of canter poles. Most riders do not like riding over canter poles as it makes their stride absolutely committed – they have no chance to adjust the stride – so we use the canter poles for that precise reason. It is very easy to allow the short-striding horse to shorten his stride still further because that is comfortable, but when you ask him to lengthen his stride it can be uncomfortable.

Place the canter poles 10ft (3.05m) apart. This encourages the horse to make a slightly lengthened stride between each pole. As time goes on you can widen the distance between the poles slightly, up to a distance of 10ft 6ins (3.20m), to produce a fairly ideal, bold stride that is ready to take on bigger fences. You may scratch your head and say, 'Well, earlier he said that an ideal stride is 12ft long, and here he is saying that a 10ft 6ins stride is ideal – something doesn't add up somewhere!' Well, the horse will spend a little time in the air, step forward boldly and land fairly close to the poles, making the stride nearer to 11ft (3.35m) than 10ft 6ins (3.20m).

Remember that you are trying to adjust your horse **by degrees**, so it would be very foolish of you to place the poles 12ft (3.65m) apart when your horse has a 9ft (2.65m) stride. Be content to see your horse lengthen from a 9ft (2.65m) to an 11ft (3.35m) stride, which is a stride sufficiently long enough to get you through combinations. Once your horse has accepted that he is able to lengthen his stride when required and you are comfortable riding him through those lengthened strides, the rest of the adjustment needed to make 12ft (3.65m) strides will be created by the horse's natural enthusiasm and by the adrenaline rush once in the ring. You are not making it a normal thing for your short-striding horse to go through every distance on a long stride; you are simply creating an element of adjustment that may be necessary occasionally through the horse's jumping career. You are trying to change the horse's habit of going short into a habit of being adjustable.

Once you are cantering between your original two poles and are easily able to shorten or lengthen your horse's stride as much as is practically possible, it is time to raise the poles to create two small jumps of approximately 18ins (approximately 45cm) to make the task into a jumping exercise. The important thing to remember now is: **do not change anything in your approach.** As you become confident with the poles at 18ins (45cm) then you can begin to increase the complexity of the exercise by gradually increasing the height of the poles, by changing the related distance, by introducing oxers and spreads and by adding a double combination to the end of the related distance.

Now is the time to put your homework to the test by putting several of your different exercises together. You can do this in a field when the going underfoot is good or in a 20m (66ft) x 60m (196ft) arena. You could, say, construct a three-stride distance to a four-stride distance then have a curved line to a five-stride distance with, perhaps, a double at the end. Then you can come back over the same course, having your double combination as your first fence. All the time you are educating yourself to ride as clearly and as positively as you can to the level, measured distance, but you should always be acutely aware that if your horse falters or makes a mistake you must be ready to adjust his stride so that he arrives at the next fence in balance.

If you are riding from an oxer to a vertical, you will have to approach the oxer with a little more power, and you are going to have to be ready to make a quick adjustment to your horse's stride as soon as he has landed. Because the vertical is less imposing your horse will be less likely to respect it and more likely to take off too close, taking out the top rail with his front legs. To make him respect the vertical you have to make a shortening adjustment to his stride and you will have to prepare mentally for that adjustment while you are in the air.

In the reverse, if you are riding from a vertical to an oxer, you will approach the vertical with caution and a slightly slower stride. Then you will need to put an enormous amount of power into the first stride after landing so that the horse is moving forward with sufficient activity in his stride and sufficient enthusiasm in his mind to jump the oxer.

All of these exercises need to be practised time and time again *before* you go your first show, not after you have made your first big mistakes in public. Related distance riding need not be that awful thing that you sometimes see, where the rider attacks the fences blindly and storms through the distance regardless of what it is. If you can make your horse confident through training, he will eventually teach himself that a related distance is easy to go to and jump, and will not get into a state of panic about it. **Gaining your horse's confidence can take many months; losing it can take seconds.**

# CHAPTER 12

# Jumping Combinations

Many years ago, in novice competitions the only double combination you came across was a double of uprights. It was there just to introduce the horse to the idea of jumping two fences together. But over the years, as riders, horses, technique and training have improved and people are more capable, even at a very novice level you are usually expected to jump up to two double combinations consisting of oxers, triple bars or uprights.

The combinations that you will encounter most frequently are either double combinations, made up of two obstacles with a distance of no more than 36ft (10.95m) between them, or treble combinations, with a distance of no more than 36ft (10.95m) between them. In some exceptional circumstances, competitions contain quadruple combinations, made up of four obstacles with a distance of no more than 36ft (10.95m) between them.

The approach to any combination requires all the ingredients that we have already talked about in our work on the flat – rhythm, impulsion, balance, and correct speed. It also requires calmness. (See photos opposite.)

The distances between elements in a combination are formulaic: maximum and minimum distances for any given combination at any height are set down in the BSJA Coursebuilders' Manual. Nearly every coursebuilder sets out to build a good combination – to build a 'trick' combination would be to lay themselves wide

open to accusations of purposely setting out to maim and destroy the confidence of the horses. How each horse covers the set distance will vary greatly, dependent on several factors. Muddy conditions, an uphill slope, a cramped arena and jumping away from home can shorten a horse's stride by up to 1ft (30cm). Springy turf, jumping towards home, a gentle downhill slope and a spacious arena can lengthen the stride by the same amount. Even the colour of the combination may have an effect on how it is jumped, so it is vital to watch other riders and see how their horses cope with the distances.

One of the greatest mistakes that people make when jumping combinations is to believe that the faster they go, the more likely they are to come out the other side. Unfortunately all that really happens is that the horse becomes more and more unbalanced and the usual result is a heavy shower of dislodged poles! If, because of your anxiety, your horse comes to the first fence in a long, flat, hurried stride then he will take off in a low, long trajectory, and whether or not he lowers a pole he will land on his forehand. He then has only one or two strides in which to pick himself up ready to jump the next fence. If he is already travelling too fast and heavily onto his forehand, he is going to have a severe problem getting himself organised and back onto his hocks to jump the second fence, and the problems are going to be greatly multiplied if there is a third element.

The golden rule is that you cannot jump out until

**Combination jumping.** A young horse moves effortlessly through a large double combination.

you have jumped in. 'Of course you can't jump out until you jump in!' comes the universal cry, but my point is that you cannot jump out in balance unless you have jumped in in balance. So initially you must address the problem of the 'in' part of the combination.

Presumably you have walked the course before attempting to jump it, so you know the distance between the fences – if you do not then you are leaving yourself open to problems that should have been avoided. As you pace the distance out between the fences you should also assess the type of combination you will be jumping: for example, is it a vertical to an oxer, an oxer to a vertical, or a triple bar to an oxer to a vertical. Your approach to the combination should correspond with whatever the 'going in' part is, whether it be a vertical or an oxer. What happens after that you have to deal with as it happens.

A double or treble combination is just a very short related distance so how you jump the 'in' part will directly relate to how you jump the next one or two parts.

The big oxer will be even 'bigger' as a part of a combination because the horse will see the fence behind it and will be backing off the first fence, so you will have to approach the fence with a small increase of pace and a large increase in activity. Knowing that the fence is coming, you need to build the canter and adjust the stride to suit the particular fence you are approaching. Hopefully the coursebuilder will have taken this into account and made the distance between the two fences short enough to allow the horse to back off, land a little steeply and short and still make the distance to the second fence.

I try to stress to my riders that they should know on the way to the fence how their horse is feeling. One or two strides away they should be able to tell whether he is going forward and is taking the fence on or is backing off and withdrawing his labour. You must react to these feelings as quickly as possible, so if you feel the horse backing off the combination you must inject a little more enthusiasm into his stride so that you know that he is moving into your hand. It is always better to have your horse taking you to the fence than having to kick. He should not be pulling your arms out, but he should, at least, be as enthusiastic about getting to the fence as you are, or, better, twice as keen as you are!

**Jumping a training combination.** Here the trotting pole is placed 9ft (2.65m) away from the first fence. This encourages the horse to lower his head and become balanced. It also helps him to arrive at the first fence in the right place to take off. The canter poles are 9ft (2.65m) away from the following fences. Always measure canter poles from the fence to be jumped. This ensures a safe distance and prevents the horse from treading on the pole. By keeping the one-stride-to-one-stride combination simple you encourage the horse to jump in balance, in rhythm and in control.

There is nothing worse than coming to a fence when you are full of enthusiasm but knowing that your horse has no zest for the job. You will end up approaching the fence kicking and kicking, and thinking 'Oh, my God, this is going to be a complete disaster!' On the other hand if your horse is moving forward and feeling enthusiastic, you ride to the fence thinking, 'This feels good,' and you know that you'll be able to deal with almost anything.

Once you are 'in' you will know what you have to do to get out, but before you reach that point you will spend a few milliseconds travelling through the air. As the horse takes off you can assess the take-off; and as he

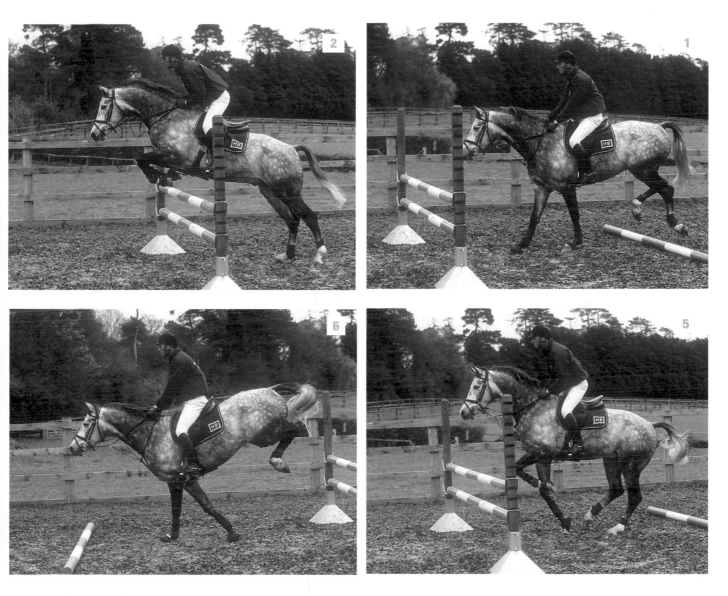

clears the fence you can assess the shape of jump the horse has created and where you are going to land. If you think, 'Yes, that was a good take-off … this is a good jump and we are going to land in the right spot,' then there is little else to do to prepare for the next jump. But if you think, 'Help, we are going to land short,' then you know you are going to have to kick. If, however, you think, 'We are going to land too near to the next fence,' then you know that you are going to have to take a pull. You have to react when you have jumped the fence, but you must **know** that you must react **before** you land – your brain has to be working ahead. The more quickly you think, the more time you have in which to react. I

liken it to skidding on ice, whether in a car or on a bicycle. Suddenly everything seems to go into slow motion, but that isn't reality – the world is not slowing down, but your brain is speeding up; it overtakes the situation and plans your reactions.

Treble combinations do not take any more jumping than do double combinations, but your horse may back off more, daunted by seeing so many poles and so much colour in front of him. In novice competitions the combination should always encourage the horse to jump. An ascending oxer to a vertical is the most inviting combination, as opposed to a square oxer to a vertical or a vertical to an oxer. A sensible coursebuilder will put the filler on the first element of a combination, but you do get bad course designers who will put the filler under the second or third elements and use poles on the first fence. This will direct the horse's eye straight through the poles to the filler, encouraging him to ignore the first element – not good, especially for a novice horse.

When it comes to training your horse to jump combinations, like everything else related to training your horse, keep it simple. Make everything very straight forward at home so that at no time does the horse suffer knock-backs. The important thing to do is to give your horse things to do that he can cope with easily, so that he will come back for more. If you keep asking him to do the impossible he is very likely to throw down his tools. However, you must be progressive.

All young horses jump very differently. Some will be very cautious and green and will jump very high with gangly, dangling legs, others will be a lot braver and will carry on regardless so that by the time you reach the fourth fence you are flying. The brave horse may be easier to train through combinations but he may not always leave every fence standing. The cautious, careful horse that is loath to touch a fence may take more time and be more difficult to train through combinations, but he is going to clear them.

I start by building small lines of three or four fences approximately 18ins (45cm) high so that the horse gets used to seeing a line of jumps. Once he is happy you can start to build wider and higher. It is important to be careful with the distances because you must not make any distance so long that the horse begins to flatten nor so short that he is tempted to bounce between each fence. When you are building small combinations you should ensure that the distance between each fence will

encourage your horse to make a nice, rounded jump over each obstacle. Vary the fences between one-stride (23 ft/7m) and two-stride (33ft 6ins/10.20m) distances.

As the height of the fences increases so should the distance between them. A rule of thumb is to increase the distance by 6ins (15cm) for every 6ins (15cm) of height, but always take your conditions into account. Mud, and jumping uphill can shorten your horse's stride by up to 1ft (30cm), whereas good turf and gentle downhill slopes can increase it by the same amount. Jumping towards or away from home and the amount of space you are jumping in can also affect length of stride.

Start by building your line of fences purely with poles. I like to introduce fillers at the sides of the jumps, acting much as a wing. This way the horse gets used to seeing them without actually having to jump them. As his confidence grows they can gradually be moved in towards the centre of the fence.

If your horse is very bold and is running through the line of fences, getting closer and closer to each fence, then put a pole in between each fence to encourage him to draw his eye down to the ground so that he makes a deliberate stride and is in a better position to jump the fence. You do not want masses of poles on the floor for a timid horse, though, as it is likely to make him more anxious. However, as the timid horse becomes more forward-going then I would put the poles on the floor and lengthen the distances between each fence to encourage him to move forward through the distance. The pole should be measured from the jump you are going to jump, not the one you are jumping. (See diagrams below.)

Do not be tempted **not** to start with the basics with your tremendously talented, scopey horse just because he *is* tremendously talented and scopey. **All** horses will eventually 'hit a wall', and once you hit that wall it is incredibly difficult to get over unless you have done the groundwork. If the horse is not completely happy about jumping three or four fences in a row and can take

**Safe distances for canter poles.** Always measure canter poles backwards from the first rail of the fence you are jumping never forwards from the fence you have jumped.

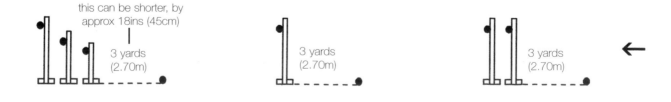

those jumps well within his stride, then when you do meet a problem such as a difficult combination your horse is going to be so frightened that he will be backing off before you jump the first fence. On the other hand, if you have done all your homework he may hesitate and take a look, but the basic idea in his head will be to go forward and take on the jump.

Always remember that speed is not the answer, although it is a trap that we all fall into at one time or another. I remember riding a young horse through a treble combination and as he approached the third element he ran out, although he had been backing off during the approach. I brought him towards the combination a second time with a lot more speed and in fact

he backed off more and he still ran out. The answer to a problem like that is to doff your hat, retire, and go home and practise – the horse was not ready to jump that particular combination.

Another mistake that a large number of riders make is to bully their horse through combinations when the horse is just not ready to jump them. If your horse is making mistakes through combinations, it does not necessarily mean that he needs to be punished. Often, horses make mistakes in combinations because they are genuinely frightened, and if you hit a horse for being frightened it will just increase the fear. Once a horse gets 'combination phobia' he has only to turn a corner and see a combination and he's back-pedalling.

# CHAPTER 13

# Gymnastic Jumping

Gymnastic exercises are very important and will teach you and your horse several things. For example, jumping a grid on a school-master can help the rider's confidence, balance and position; whilst the primary function of gymnastic work for the horse is to improve his technique. These exercises will also develop the horse's gymnastic ability and power. It is vital, though, to aim the exercises at the level of skill that the horse has attained.

Beware, grids can also be something of an easy option for a coach. Too often a show jumping lesson can turn into just a gridwork session, and overdoing gridwork is just as retrograde a step as not doing any at all.

## Using ground lines

Ground-line poles should be used under every fence to encourage your horse to look down to the base of the jump and to discourage him from running in too close. It is a misconception that a ground line frightens the horse off the pole or actively encourages him to stand off too much. When jumping verticals the ground line should always be at least 1ft (30 cm) in front of the jump, and as the fences get higher it can be pulled out further.

When jumping oxers the ground-line pole needs to be underneath the front rail and should only be pulled out occasionally if the horse needs to be encouraged to back off. Always place ground lines in front of or under the fence, never behind it. A false ground line will trick your horse into thinking he must take off closer to the fence than he actually needs to, possibly leading to a nasty accident and almost certainly to a loss of confidence. Also remember that the more poles you use in a grid the more daunting and difficult it may look to your horse. Confronted with such a maze of poles your horse may either misjudge where to put his feet or may just decide to go on strike.

## Effective gymnastic exercises

Here is a very simple exercise for a horse at the beginning of his career. It is aimed at teaching him to go from one fence to another with enthusiasm and confidence. Put a placing pole or three trotting poles in front of a small fence, and then set up another small jump a short distance (approximately 21ft/6.40m) away. This exercise draws the horse's eye to the floor, makes him look where he is putting his feet, and asks him to take two simple jumps. When the horse is comfortable jumping these two fences you can place a back rail on the second part, creating an oxer. This encourages the horse to make a bigger leap which will launch him into the air, and soon he will realise that he can actually jump a bigger fence.

As he becomes more confident, you can raise the second element and begin to draw the front bar gradu-

**A simple schooling grid.** Having negotiated three trotting poles, the horse jumps a small vertical and canters confidently over a pole placed 9ft (2.65m) away from the front rail of an oxer. The distance between the vertical and the front rail of the oxer is 21ft (6.3m). As your horse improves in balance and strength, you can raise the height of the oxer and widen it by moving the front rail towards the vertical. Remember to move the canter pole backwards by the same distance. Eventually this exercise can be superseded by the Power Grid (see next page).

ally towards the first element, thus widening the oxer and shortening the distance between the two fences. (See photo sequence above.)

Taking this exercise to its ultimate, as it would be jumped by a very experienced horse, the highest I would make the oxer would be approximately 3ft 7ins (1.10m), and the distance between the two fences would shorten to 15ft (4.55m) making the spread 6ft (1.85m) wide – quite a considerable fence.

A similar exercise, and one of my favourites, is the

**Grid to improve general technique.** Approach in trot.

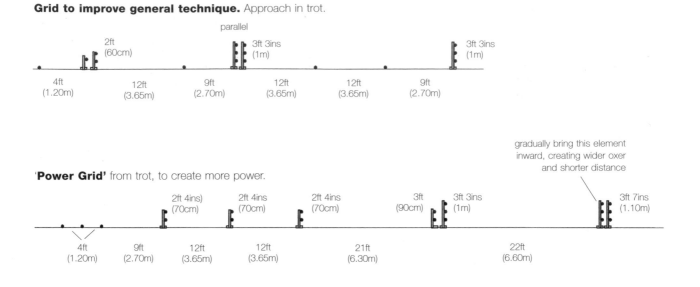

parallel

2ft (60cm)   3ft 3ins (1m)   3ft 3ins (1m)

4ft (1.20m)   12ft (3.65m)   9ft (2.70m)   12ft (3.65m)   12ft (3.65m)   9ft (2.70m)

gradually bring this element inward, creating wider oxer and shorter distance

**'Power Grid'** from trot, to create more power.

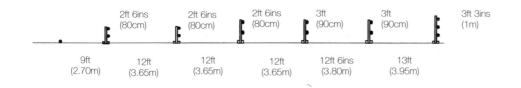

2ft 4ins) (70cm)   2ft 4ins (70cm)   2ft 4ins (70cm)   3ft (90cm)   3ft 3ins (1m)   3ft 7ins (1.10m)

4ft (1.20m)   9ft (2.70m)   12ft (3.65m)   12ft (3.65m)   21ft (6.30m)   22ft (6.60m)

**Bounce grid** from trot. Improves horse's balance, gives him confidence and sharpens his mind. Start with two fences (one bounce) and add one at a time.

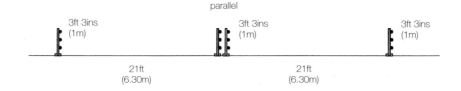

2ft 6ins (80cm)   2ft 6ins (80cm)   2ft 6ins (80cm)   3ft (90cm)   3ft (90cm)   3ft 3ins (1m)

9ft (2.70m)   12ft (3.65m)   12ft (3.65m)   12ft (3.65m)   12ft 6ins (3.80m)   13ft (3.95m)

**Canter grid** to improve your horse's front leg action. Carefully move each side of the oxer outwards, widening the oxer and reducing the distance between each fence. Move each element of the oxer a maximum of 1ft (30cm).

parallel

3ft 3ins (1m)   3ft 3ins (1m)   3ft 3ins (1m)

21ft (6.30m)   21ft (6.30m)

**Trot grid** to improve hind leg action. Note that the back rail on the second ascending oxer is much higher than the front rail.

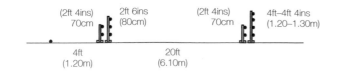

(2ft 4ins) 70cm   2ft 6ins (80cm)   (2ft 4ins) 70cm   4ft–4ft 4ins (1.20–1.30m)

4ft (1.20m)   20ft (6.10m)

**Bounce grid.** Bounce fences can be placed between 10ft (3m) and 12ft (3.65m) apart. They are an excellent exercise for increasing your horse's elasticity and sharpness of mind. They also encourage the horse to use his shoulders. Bounce exercises are hard work for your horse, so use them sparingly.

Power Grid. It simply consists of three bounce fences, followed by one non-jumping stride to a fourth vertical, and then a further non-jumping stride to either a square oxer or an descending oxer. (Although not used in competition the descending oxer is a useful and legitimate training aid that encourages the horse to be neater and sharper with his front legs.)

Both the above exercises should be undertaken with caution, but they have two major effects. One, they improve the shoulder action and bascule; and two, they encourage power jumping off the hind leg in a short distance. We are, in fact, condensing the stride to jump the width, not increasing it.

## Bounce jumping

I also use bounce jumping quite frequently, either from trot or from canter. A bounce distance is one in which

**Jumping a bounce combination.** Here the horse has jumped five consecutive bounces. Do not make your bounce grid with more than six fences – to do so would be unproductive and would cause unnecessary wear and tear on your horse.

the horse has to take off for the second fence with his front feet before his hind feet have touched the ground, obviously entailing an enormous amount of power, drive and athleticism.

Bounce jumping is an exercise that used to be looked down on in the show jumping fraternity but it is becoming more popular as its benefits are more widely understood. It makes the horse think very quickly, so it is a good exercise for his mind, and because he has to move very quickly, it is also a good exercise for his body. His shoulders have to come up very quickly, and, as a result, his head has to go down quickly. As his shoulders go up and his neck goes down, his back comes up in the middle, which allows him to throw his hind legs away from the fence in a correct manner. All in all, the bounce causes an awful lot of hinges, pulleys and levers to work very quickly in rapid succession.

The bounce fence can be very small, say, 1ft 6ins (0.45m) to 2ft (0.60m) for a young horse, or as high as 3ft 4ins (1m) for the more experienced horse. Try to imagine the strength and gymnastic ability required by a horse to bounce over a row of four or five fences at

that height. Do not make the distance between each bounce any less than 12ft (3.65m) unless the fences are very small. To make a bounce overly short puts too much strain on the horse's joints, muscles and tendons. Start off with two or three very small bounce fences in a row, but always take care with bounce fences because the horse can get confused and intimidated by a barrage of poles.

A timid horse may jump two or three bounces happily, but if confronted with two or three more he may start panicking – touching a foot down in the wrong place or tripping over the fences. For such a timid horse you could make the fences even smaller, using poles raised 6ins (15cm) off the ground – anything to make training simple, inviting and painless.

## General rules for creating a grid

- Do not put a bounce fence in the middle or at the end of a mixed grid.
- Build a grid that is within the capability of both the rider and the horse.
- Distances that are made slightly short encourage a horse to jump off his hocks – which is good.
- Distances that are too long make a horse jump flat and throw him onto his forehand – that is bad!
- If you want to make a bold horse more careful you

**Canter grid** to improve the horse's scope. It is designed for an experienced horse. You can gradually widen the final oxer by moving both elements.

**Canter grid** using three raised poles. To improve the horse's 'vertical' jumping ability.

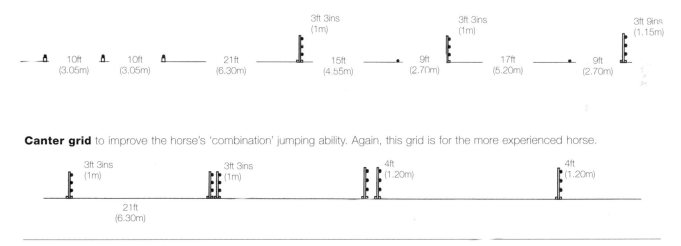

**Canter grid** to improve the horse's 'combination' jumping ability. Again, this grid is for the more experienced horse.

can increase the number of obstacles in your grid.

- To provide a horse with one non-jumping stride between fences the distance should be between 23ft 6ins (7.15m) and 26ft (7.90m).
- To provide a horse with two non-jumping strides between fences the distance should be between 34ft (10.45m) and 35ft 6ins (10.80m).
- The distance between two vertical fences can be shorter than the distance between a vertical and an oxer or than between two oxers.
- Build your grid in a straight line.
- Always have an experienced person on the ground: (a) checking your distances, and (b) rebuilding knocked down fences.
- If you are using trotting poles, make sure, if at all possible, that they are stabilised in wooden blocks. If they are not, keep a sharp eye on them to make sure they are not moved.
- Trotting poles should be approximately 4ft 6ins (1.35m) apart when used as an approach to a grid, but they do need to be adjusted to suit the horse's gait.

- Trotting poles used on their own should be approximately 4ft 6ins (1.35m) or 9ft (2.70m) apart.
- Canter poles on the approach to the grid should be 10ft (3.05m) apart and should also, if possible, be stabilised in wooden blocks. The last canter pole should be 9ft (2.70m) from the first fence.

Finally, remember that any tool you can use to keep the rider and the horse safe is a good idea – the fewer mistakes you make, the quicker you learn. Good practice develops confidence, while making bad mistakes or letting people do unsafe or unwise things does not develop confidence. Attempting to teach your horse to show jump through trickery will not work, but providing him with a large knowledge base gives him plenty to fall back on; it gives him the opportunity to be confident with something familiar. If you are training the horse with good gymnastic exercises at home and you make a mistake at a show you can come home and go through familiar exercises to rebuild his confidence.

**Good practice makes perfect.**

# CHAPTER 14

# Ditches and Water

Some coursebuilders like to include ditches, water trays, and even water jumps. Your aim should be to introduce your horse to all of these different obstacles in a schooling situation before he meets them in the competition arena. I jump my young horses over small ditches and water jumps from a very early age, so that they are not perturbed by them when they encounter them at a later date. Do not assume that a spooky, flighty horse is going to have a big problem with ditches and water – some of my hottest horses have taken to these obstacles like ducks to water, while calmer and steadier horses have hated the whole idea of going near a hole in the ground – perhaps they were worried I might bury them there!

Start by introducing your horse to a water tray. This can be a narrow wooden tray painted blue, a blue tarpaulin or even a split, blue plastic fertiliser bag held down securely with poles. If your horse approaches and jumps the water tray as if he has been jumping them all his life, and he clears it out of his stride, you are unlikely ever to have problems. If he spooks a little, runs past it or stops a couple of times but is then willing to jump it, and later to jump it with more and more confidence, once again you are unlikely to have problems in the future.

The horse that **is** difficult is the one with whom you spend the entire morning trying to get him **near** the tray, and the entire afternoon trying to get him over it, only to find that he is just as unwilling the next day, the

day after and the day after that. My own feelings are that if after five or six days the horse still does not want to know, you have big problems that may prove insurmountable. True, you may, in time, at least get the horse over the obstacle, but you are unlikely ever to be able to trust him in a competition situation, where he will quickly learn that if you cannot get him over the tray within three attempts he does not have to have another go.

At home, I use the lunge line and an experienced, calm helper to get my horses used to ditches. I attach the lunge line to the horse in the same manner that I use when lungeing – i.e. through one bit ring, over the poll and attached to the other bit ring. Then I walk with the horse up to a small ditch, step over the ditch myself and stand on the landing side, with the horse standing on the take-off side. It is now up to my helper to coax the horse to step over the ditch. To do this, the helper uses the voice and the lunge whip laid gently against the horse's hocks. Very soon the horse is likely to put in an

---

**Introducing water at home** (opposite).

(1) Leading a horse calmly towards the water tray. (2) The trainer steps over the water – this shows the horse that there is nothing to fear. (3) The trainer waits, allowing the horse to see the water and investigate it. (4) The horse is gently encouraged to step or jump over the water. (5) Success! (6) The horse canters confidently over the water from the lunge.(7) A pole is introduced to teach the horse to jump and gain height over the fence.

**Simulating water.** Polythene makes a good 'water' jump if you haven't the facilities to make a real one.

**Tackling water.** Poles over the 'water' will encourage the horse to gain height.

impressive leap over the gulf. Standing on the landing side, I have to be pretty quick-witted so as not to be squashed beyond recognition, but the horse does give you warning that he is about to take the plunge. For this exercise to be successful and safe, the ditch used must have guardrails on either side to prevent the horse from running out and to stop the lunge rein from snagging.

When the horse has jumped the ditch, and you have given him **plenty** of pats and praise, you can start the process over again. Once your horse has learnt that the troll in the ditch is not going to leap out and grab him by the legs, he will find the whole experience a great deal of fun. As he gains confidence, you can jump him over the ditch whilst lungeing him on a circle, before jumping the ditch from his back. You can use the same procedure for jumping small water jumps and small banks.

## Golden rules for jumping natural obstacles

• Start small and simple.
• Make sure there is someone on the ground to help you and to reassure your horse.
• Jump as many different obstacles in as many different surroundings as you can.

• Be progressive.
• The more confidence and experience your horse gains outside the arena, the more confidence he will have inside the arena.

Ask your local show centre if you can school over their natural obstacles on a non-show day. Most are willing

**Make it easy.** A good, visible ground line is helpful when teaching a horse to jump water.

**Here, mum, have you seen what's down there?** If you haven't done your homework your horse is unlikely to clear the first water tray he sees.

**Natural hedge.** Expect to meet the occasional natural hedge in a competition. Make sure your horse meets a good variety of natural obstacles before you start competing.

to hire out their facilities. If possible, take your coach with you so that he can help you through any crisis and keep you level-headed. If you cannot take your coach, be sure to take an experienced helper. In years gone by a season's hunting was almost obligatory for the young show jumper and this introduced him to a huge variety of natural obstacles. It also taught him to move on boldly and to attack the fences. Sadly, most modern hunting country has been divided by barbed-wire fences and relies entirely on narrow hunt jumps.

Hunter trials are a good modern alternative, but you do need to go to an event where the fences are well constructed out of good, solid timber. Bold fences will encourage your horse to jump in a more natural way and to enjoy his jumping. Badly positioned, flimsy fences will not help your horse in any way, so ask your coach, local riding club or knowledgeable friends about courses which have a good reputation. UK Chaser courses can be found throughout Britain and these provide a large variety of fences set around farmland. Usually the courses are approximately eight miles long and the fences vary from 2ft (60cm) to 3ft 3ins (1m) in height. These courses are professionally built and you can school over the fences rather than compete over them if you wish.

**Hunter trials.** To compete in hunter trials you will need to wear a body protector. Many cross country practice courses will insist that you do.

# Show Jumping Competitions

Show jumping can be divided into four levels of competition:
(1) unaffiliated show jumping,
(2) affiliated show jumping at novice level,
(3) affiliated show jumping at intermediate level, and
(4) show jumping at Grand Prix and international level.

## Unaffiliated or unrecognised show jumping competitions

Horses and riders jumping in this category of competition do not have to be registered with any governing body, nor do the organisers or the officials. The competitions do not adhere to any particular rules and there are no limiting heights of jumps. One big draw-back to this section of the sport is that as there is no governing body there are no official judging or course building standards. It is also prey to pot-hunters: people on older, more experienced horses that have no particular aims or ambitions other than to win trophies, ribbons and the limited amount of prize money offered at such competitions.

For the more dedicated show jumper these shows still have their uses. They will produce a fairly calm, sensible horse that is ready to step up to affiliated shows. They are also a good arena for the novice rider to start honing his skills before moving on to greater things. Finally, unaffiliated competitions will allow you to gauge whether or not your horse has got what it takes to become a show jumper before you invest in registration – also whether show jumping is for you or not.

Many venues that stage affiliated shows will also run one or two unaffiliated classes before they run their affiliated classes. Try to take your horse to these venues because you know that the fences used and the courses built will be up to a recognised standard. A show jumping course built by a person who is not aware of the technical intricacies of course design is likely to damage your horse's confidence as he tries to make impossible distances and unreasonable turns.

## Novice show jumping under affiliated or recognised rules

To anybody who has an ambition to show jump and thinks they have the ability and determination to do so, my words of advice are: go ahead and do it properly – register with your country's governing association, which in Britain is the British Show Jumping Association (BSJA). Once you have done so you will never look back and you will never regret it. The much enhanced courses you will meet will certainly improve you and your horse, and the stiffer competition should make you try harder.

It is a very big step up, if not physically at least mentally. Jumping under BSJA rules means that you will be riding against some professional riders at shows often held at professional venues. The courses you jump may

**Competition fences.** The fences and courses at recognised events will be well built and well made.

**Competition riding.** A young rider at the start of her career, competing in a Junior Novice class.

not be bigger than the ones you have been jumping at local shows but they **will seem** to be. A well-built course, full of colour, using lots of good poles and fillers will look quite imposing. The standard of jumps used in BSJA, or in recognised competitions of any federation, is invariably better than those used at unrecognised shows.

In general, the whole set-up at an affiliated show will be safer and more professional than at a local, unofficial show. The access and parking space will be more acceptable; and the riding surface should be even and, on the whole, better prepared. The courses will be built by an approved coursebuilder, and official judges, well versed

**Competition riding.** (above left) Taking part in a Foxhunter class. (above right) Junior Rider jumping at the highest level.

**Competition riding.** Competing in an Area International Trial.

**Competition riding.** This rider is competing at the highest level – for his country.

in the rules and in safety procedures, will oversee the entire event.

Shows recognised by the BSJA offer a wide range of competitions for every grade of horse:

• At the starting level there are classes of 2ft 9ins to 3ft (approx. 0.90m). Classes then rise progressively in height right through to International Trials, which are 5ft (1.55m).

• The height of jumps used in the first round of the Novice and Preliminary classes must not exceed 3ft (0.90m) The course will include two double combinations, but will not feature a treble or a water jump.

• At the second round of a Novice Qualifier the fences will be up to 3ft 3$\frac{1}{2}$ins (1m) and again, although there are two double combinations there will be no treble or water jump.

• In the Junior Preliminary classes the jumps will be up to 2ft 6ins (0.85m) in the first round and up to 3ft 3$\frac{1}{2}$ins (1m) in the second round. For the Seniors the speed is set at 325m per minute and in Junior competitions it is 300m per minute.

• The height of jumps used in the first round of Senior Newcomers Preliminary classes will not exceed 3ft 9$\frac{1}{2}$ins (1.15m). In these classes you will come up against your first treble combination and may be asked to jump a water tray. A small water jump – not exceeding 8ft 4ins (2.5m) may be included, as long as there is a straightforward alternative fence. In Junior

Newcomers Preliminary classes you will not be expected to jump a treble combination or a water jump. The fences will not exceed 3ft 3$\frac{1}{2}$ins (1m) and in the Regional Finals, 3ft 9$\frac{1}{2}$ins (1.15m). Again, the speed set for the Seniors is 325m per minute and for Juniors 300m a minute.

• The jump-off course in any class will be raised by a minimum of 2$\frac{1}{2}$ins (5cm), and at least two fences will be raised by a maximum of 5ins (10cm). Fences in combinations may not necessarily be raised at all.

Other classes such as the 'Foxhunter' series and Grade C competitions are still considered 'novice' classes but they do ask some more questions for the true amateur and are really better described as 'intermediate' classes. For those less experienced riders who have obtained a schoolmaster on which to learn their trade, the BSJA Member's Cup is an invaluable competition. It allows riders who are not in the top two hundred on the national computer rankings to compete on horses of any grade. In the first round of this competition the fences will not exceed 3ft 9$\frac{1}{2}$ins (1.15m). Many shows also host amateur owner competitions which allow like-minded people to compete among themselves.

Every country will have their own equivalent to these classes and the rules are usually similar. This category could be considered the 'make or break' stage

**Jos Lansink**

66 It is very difficult to get to the top – and when you get there it is even more difficult to stay there! You need not one good horse but several, and you also need supportive owners or sponsors. To get to the top takes a lot of work, a lot of training and a lot of self-belief – especially when things are not going right for you. 99

where you can make the big decision to 'step up' to the intermediate levels or to decide 'I am comfortable where I am.'

## Affiliated or recognised jumping at Intermediate level

By the time you are jumping courses of 3ft 11ins (1.20m) and above in classes such as Foxhunter, National Grade C and perhaps even National Grade B classes, you are jumping more seriously challenging courses. All of these courses will include a treble combination and may include water trays and water jumps. These competitions are the ultimate aim of many riders and they are contested by serious and talented amateurs rubbing shoulders with top international riders bringing on their future stars. It is not impossible to compete at this level of competition as an amateur rider but it is

a lot more difficult for an amateur to win.

Young riders (ages 16 to 21) competing in this range of competition will be expected to jump anything up to 4ft 9ins (1.45m) and juniors up to age 16 will be expected to jump courses of approximately 4ft 3ins (1.30m).

The speed that you will be required to travel at in these competitions will range from 325 metres per minute in the Foxhunter and Grade C competitions, to 350 metres per minute in the Grade B competitions. Thus you will gradually have to learn to increase your horse's tempo, and to walk courses carefully, finding places to shave off valuable metres.

## Jumping at international level

This is it – the ultimate challenge. This level includes International competitions, International Trials and Olympic Starspotters competitions. The jumps in the first rounds of these competitions may be up to 5ft (1.50m). Most proficient riders will ultimately feel comfortable jumping at up to 4ft 3ins (1.30m) but many will rapidly start to struggle above that height. The top echelons of any sport are hard to reach, but this should not put off anyone trying to break through. If we did not have young, dedicated and ambitious riders chipping away at the 'big boys' then the sport would soon die.

Skill, financial support, an ability to stay calm under pressure and an indomitable, insatiable desire to win are all-important at this standard. Riders who compete at this level are totally self-motivated and doggedly self-disciplined. If you fit that description then the sky is your limit.

# CHAPTER 16

# Going to a Show

Before you even think about going to a show you need to go through the following checklist and make sure that you are able to say 'yes' to everything:

- Is your horse obedient to your aids?
- Is he fit?
- Are *you* fit?
- Are you feeding good quality feed appropriate to the work he is doing?
- Is he fat and flabby or sleek and well muscled?
- Are his teeth, feet and back in a healthy state?
- Is he fully sound with no hint of encroaching spavin or splint?
- Is he totally free of virus, cough or runny nose?
- Is his worming and vaccination regime up to date?
- Do your saddle and bridle (including the bit) fit correctly, and are they safe, and clean?
- Is all your auxiliary equipment (brushing boots, rugs, headcollars, etc.) clean and safe?
- Is your horse not too fresh? (A really fresh horse is not likely to perform at his best, as he will be too fizzy to do so.)

If you *can* say 'yes' to everything then you need have no worries about taking your horse to a show because he is in good health and ready for action. The point that I am trying to make is that horses do not become nappy and bad tempered just because they want to, it is nearly always because they have been pushed beyond their capabilities or have been asked to do something when they are not fit to do it. Horses and riders have only the talent, mentally and physically, that they are born with. If you recognise and accept these limitations it is almost guaranteed that you will make progress.

The biggest mistake you can make on the morning of a show is to get up late and rush around. Remember when you went on holiday and left everything to the last minute? Can you recall the panic that you felt running to the check-out? Well, the panic your horse feels as you run about getting in a flap is greater because he has no idea *why* you are getting in a flap. If you are lucky enough to have a brilliant groom you may be able to stay in bed, but nobody I ever worked for did that – they were too concerned about their horse's welfare to laze around until all the work was done.

It is necessary to devise a plan for every show that you go to. Remember that plans do not **always** work, but if you do not have a plan then it cannot work. Every good rider learns to adopt a system. They know what works from experience and so they always attempt to do things in the same order.

Try to work out on paper what time you need to leave. Work backward from the start of the class. Give yourself 30 minutes to warm up and to be ready, standing at the side of the collecting-ring steward, when your number is called. Take into account learning and walking the course, preparing yourself, getting tacked up (including the removal of all travelling gear and the putting on of boots and gadgets), collecting your numbers, unloading your horse, organising your crew and acquainting yourself with the show ground layout – including finding the ring in which you are going to jump!

Also think about how long it is going to take you to get to the showground, allowing time for traffic hold-ups and getting lost. At home think about how long it is going to take you to carry out your normal stable routine plus prepare you, your horse and his equipment and load up the lorry. Try to get as much done as possible the day before the show and give yourself an extra 30 minutes at the end of your timetable to allow for hitches. Try to err on the generous side with your timings: things always seem to take longer than you think, especially if you are riding a young horse who has now turned into an uncaged lion and you are so nervous that you are all fingers and thumbs!

Have a separate list of things you need to take. Three separate lists of what you, your horse and your lorry will need to have will help you to keep things simple. Tick off items as they are put in the lorry. As you go to more and more shows you will become more naturally organised and less dependent on your lists. One day you may not even need a written list, but take heed, there is nothing more galling than putting in all the hard work necessary to get to a show only to find out that you cannot compete your horse because you have forgotten your riding hat. I have, over the years, forgotten everything you can forget – including the horse!

## Travelling

Before you load your horse you must ensure that he is well protected against the rigours of travelling. Whether you use specially designed protective travelling boots or bandages is up to you. Travelling boots will protect the horse from injury but provide little support, whereas stable bandages provide support and some protection. The best way to provide both support and protection is to use leg wraps and stable bandages. The benefit of using bell boots to prevent overreaching may be offset by the risk of the horse sweating underneath them, leading to soreness, especially if they are made of rubber. New materials used in the lining of bell boots have made this less of a problem.

Tails should be protected by tail bandages, and with a tail guard attached to the roller. Tail bandages should be tied below the dock.

Remembering that your lorry is well ventilated, it is a good idea to travel in a warm rug. Modern thermal rugs are excellent. They are warm, and they wick moisture from the horse's body (sweat) to the outside of the rug. During the winter I might put a woollen day rug over a thermal rug once the horse has arrived at the show and is standing around. If it is an exceptionally hot day I use a light rug or no rug at all, but still with a roller for the tail guard. Poll guards are a sensible precaution if you are travelling in a trailer, but are less essential if you are travelling in a purpose-built lorry.

To guarantee that your horse arrives at the show in a relaxed state make sure that his journey is as stress-free as possible. If your horse travels badly he will lose weight and condition as he sweats up. He will become stressed and tense, possibly leading to panic and injury.

You do not need a £250,000 pantechnicon with a Jacuzzi, sauna, satellite dish and air-conditioning to travel your horse in safety and comfort, but you do need a reliable, well-ventilated lorry or trailer which is in

**Ready to go.** This horse is suitably dressed for safe travel.

**Transport.** A safe, welcoming lorry which is clean and tidy.

good condition.

There used to be a great fuss made that the horse had to travel facing away from the engine, so that if the brakes had to be applied suddenly the horse would sit on his bottom rather than plunge forward. My opinion is that a horse will get used to travelling in any direction as long as he feels safe and has enough room to spread his legs if he needs to.

Ensure that the footing in your lorry/trailer is safe, likewise the footing on the ramp. Rubber matting is an ideal, slip-free surface. Have your lorry or trailer serviced regularly – this includes renewing wooden floorboards when appropriate. A horse falling through the floor when travelling is obviously an extremely traumatic experience, not only for the horse but also for the driver, not to mention the driver of the car behind! Yes – it has happened.

Tie your horses short enough that they cannot fight or get their heads over or under partitions. Make sure that each horse has enough space and adequate ventilation. **Drive sympathetically.** Drive slowly through bends and do not slam on the brakes as you hurtle towards a roundabout – slow down gradually through the gears. If you are undertaking a long journey of eight hours or more you should allow your horse rest time in which he can stretch his legs, have a small drink and perhaps a light feed. Whether or not your horse has a haynet whilst he travels is up to you. Personally I feel that horses go to shows to perform as athletes, and that they are less likely to be able to do so if they have a belly full of hay.

When you arrive at the show walk your horse around for a few minutes to stretch his legs, to nibble a blade of grass or two, to relax and to urinate. Horses do not like to urinate in the enclosed space of a lorry, and they will perform better if they have an empty bladder.

## The pressures of competing

When you arrive at a show you will face many new challenges – known more negatively as problems! The first half an hour, especially for the young horse and/or novice rider, is always the most trying. Firstly both you and your horse are going to be excited; you will be thinking about everything other than the work plan that you carefully made at home last night: and your horse will be looking everywhere other than where he is meant to be going. Your first show will always be the worst as far as nerves go because your horse will be totally overawed by all the other horses, the flags flying, the bright colours and the public address system, etc.

As I have commented before, you must ride your horse to a much higher level at home to enable you to have a cushion once you get to your first show. If the height and technicality of the jumps at the show are less than those you have been practising over at home then that is one less thing for you to worry about.

Pressure to do well is likely to change your riding

*Points to ponder...*

- *Quitters don't win. Winners don't quit.*

style – and not always for the better. Pressure to do well may come from many different directions but two in particular are: an internal (self-imposed) pressure to do well, and an external pressure to please other people. The pressure to do well as far as your own ambition is concerned can be coped with quite easily, but when this pressure comes from friends, parents, owners, sponsors or the coach, then it can start to get to you. If those pressures are not kept under control then they will directly affect your horse, because your anxieties are transmitted to him, and things will start to go wrong.

If you are with someone who is nagging you to do this or do that and is not letting you ride with your own natural flair, it will have a negative effect on the way you do things. Your natural flair has to be directed: the excitement and the adrenaline buzz of being at a show will enhance your performance as long as you can control these feelings positively. It is your job, once you are in the arena, to do your own thing. Right or wrong, good or bad, that is what you have to do.

Your coach should not argue with you about what has gone wrong or, worse still, about something that **may** go wrong. If you have an argument about something that **may** go wrong then something almost certainly **will** go wrong!

The job of the coach is to encourage and promote a good feeling of confidence and security in the mind of the pupil before the performance. After the performance the coach's job is systematically to analyse and discuss the effort, not to destroy the rider's ego in one fell swoop.

Certainly an inquest may be necessary, but it must be short, to the point and **constructive**. If the person you are with thinks intelligently about what is going on inside your head, he or she can be a boon not a curse. Train to perfection at home – in the ring, ride instinctively. This does not mean that you throw all your training and practice out of the window as soon as you enter the ring; rather, if you have trained and practised sufficiently at home, you will be able to think and ride instinctively if and when things start to go pear-shaped in the ring.

One of the best ways to start eliminating pressure is not to go to a show until you know you are ready – in fact you need to be more ready than you think you are! There is no point in going to a show on a wing and a

**Alison Firestone**

66 It is very important always to want to work hard, no matter whether you are at the top or are striving to get to the top. Nothing is ever easy, and whether you are mucking out your horse's stall, riding without your stirrups or competing in a Grand Prix, you must keep going and keep striving to get better. 99

prayer, but this does not mean that you cannot go to a small schooling show to find out where your weaknesses lie, as we have already discussed.

When my horses are young and green I will sometimes take them to a local unaffiliated show where there are no great expectations, the jumps are bland and there are no great excitements to face. The stress put on young horses when travelling them to their first few shows is often not taken seriously enough. Horses, like us, do feel stress. This stress may manifest itself in different ways, the most obvious being to break out in a sweat. How often, at shows, do you see the ramp come down and steam escaping from the lorry like a Turkish bath?

I will trot my youngsters around a 2ft (60cm) course so that I can assess how they are likely to react at larger shows later in their careers. It is quite important to find out what your horse's reaction is likely to be at a show because it gives more insight into your horse's psyche than you will ever have at home. Do not expect to jump a round of show jumps on your first visit to a show. If your horse is too excited, just let him soak up the atmosphere, become calm and then take him home. The old saying, 'All your geese are swans at home' is never so true as when you arrive at a show and find that your beautiful swan has turned rapidly into an ugly goose!

Another important way of eliminating pressure is to make sure that you don't overstretch yourself. Don't jump in at the deep end by entering a class that is too big for you and your horse's present ability. Whilst it is

**Ulrich Kirchoff**
**Olympic gold medallist**

"I have experience of the ultimate highs and lows in this sport. When I started out in my own yard things seemed to be getting better and better all the time to the point of becoming Olympic Champion – then I lost my Olympic horse, so I know how it feels to go from elation to despair, from the top to the bottom. I want to get back to the top again – I know that it means a lot of hard work, but I am determined to achieve my goal.

To succeed at the highest level you must be quiet and patient with all your horses, especially the youngsters; you must work hard, train hard and you must believe in yourself."

lovely to buy an experienced horse who can jump easily around 4ft 6ins (1.35m) courses and to take him into 3ft 9ins (1.10m) classes to gain experience and confidence, if you are riding an inexperienced horse and trying to create confidence, you must remember that confidence takes months to build and seconds to destroy. Just a few mistakes will shatter not only your horse's confidence but also your faith in yourself. You must have an ultimate goal, one that you set for yourself in the long term, albeit competing in the Olympics or in an open class at a local show. You must also have a goal which is achievable within the foreseeable future. Never make your short-term or long-term goals totally unobtainable – they must be realistic.

*Points to ponder...*

- *Winners make things happen – losers let things happen.*

## Walking the course

It is not enough just to know the direction in which you have to jump the course, and in what order the jumps come. You must walk the course thoroughly and methodically. But before you even set foot in the arena you must study the course plan so you have a basic idea of where you are going. Note the position of the entrance, the start and the finish, as well as the speed required and time allowed for each round. Obviously you do not want to hurtle around the course, but neither do you wish to incur time faults. If you see that the course is to be ridden at 350 metres per minute then you know that you will have to ride a little quicker than if the speed required is 325 metres per minute. You will have to slightly increase your speed and/or will have to ride your corners a little more economically.

Having studied the route on paper, you can begin to walk the course. This is not intended to be a pleasant stroll on a Saturday afternoon! The first course walk should give you an idea of how your horse will see the course for the first time. If you find the view frightening then you can be sure that your horse will too! If you round a corner and come face to face with a huge yellow and black oxer, with multi-striped poles, and massive fillers with great big black holes in them, and say: 'Oh help, look at that!', you can bet your bottom dollar that your horse will think exactly the same thing.

As you walk up to each fence you must think about how you are going to approach the fence, and you must be *sure* of how you are going to approach it before you get onto your horse.

Hopefully the first fence is an inviting one that will encourage you to ride towards it without fear of knocking it down easily. Occasionally you will come across coursebuilders who build an upright or a very square fence as a first fence – not very friendly, especially on a novice course – but it still has to be jumped. More usually the first fence will be an ascending oxer or a small triple bar. A cross-bar spread, which is well filled in with a brush, is a good first fence as it encourages your horse to focus his attention on the job in hand and jump well. If your horse jumps the first fence well, it will give you boundless confidence for jumping the ones that follow.

Now walk from the first fence to the second fence.

Remember your 3ft (90cm)-long paces (see page 67). Four 3ft (90cm)-long paces are equal to one of your horse's strides. Allow two paces (6ft/1.8m) from behind the base of the first fence to indicate the point where your horse will land, and two paces (6ft/1.8m) from in front of the second fence for the take-off point. Thus one of your groups of four paces between two fences is taken up by landing and taking off. The remainder of your groups of four paces are horse strides between them.

What kind of fence is the second fence? Is the distance between it and the first fence related? Is it directly in front of the first fence, or do you have to turn a corner to get to it? If the distance is on a curved line, walk between the two fences as if you are riding it – take the same route as you intend to take on your horse. Once you have arrived at the second fence turn back and see where you have come from. How has the striding worked out through your curve? If the striding seems odd go back and walk your line again. If the striding still seems odd, consider whether you ought to take a slightly longer or shorter line between the two. You may find a line which allows you to keep to your horse's regular stride pattern, or you may have to hold him on a shortened stride to get through the curve to the jump. Keep walking the line you want to take until you are quite clear in your mind where you are going to ride it.

It is not necessary to walk distances round corners or to measure strides where more than seven or eight strides are involved. There are some coaches who like to walk every distance throughout the entire course, but I feel that this just overloads the system. It also diminishes the rider's need to be a good judge and, sometimes, a good innovator.

Think about all of these things as you progress around the course. At each combination or related distance remember that:

- eight paces (yards) between two fences is equal to one non-jumping stride,
- twelve paces (yards) is equal to two non-jumping strides,
- sixteen paces (yards) is equal to three non-jumping strides, and so on.

Distances between fences can be lengthened or shortened at the whim of the coursebuilder, so as you walk

**Get to know the course.** Walk the course with and without your coach until you know how you intend to ride it.

the course try to assess how the coursebuilder intends his course to be jumped. For example: is the distance between the double thirteen paces (in which case the coursebuilder would like to see your horse moving on an open stride), or is it eleven paces (the coursebuilder would like to see your horse moving on a short bouncy stride)?

Divide the course into all the exercises you have been practising at home: e.g. straight-line related distances, curved-line related distances, single and double fences. This will take the mystery and fear out of the competition course and reduce it to familiar tasks. Walk each exercise separately using your corners to link them together, and then walk the course as a whole, still mentally dividing it into your separate sections.

Make sure you walk the course with your horse's character in mind. Is your horse likely to spook at a particular fence? If so, you will have to ride him into the fence quite strongly. Or is he likely to run at it? – in which case you are going to have to keep him on a short, bouncy stride.

Think about where each fence is in relation to the exit and the other horses – most horses will jump more freely when jumping towards 'home', but they may not be so careful. Some horses can be a little nappy when jumping away from 'home'.

Study each fence carefully. Is it an oxer, a vertical, or a triple bar? What kind of oxer is it – a square or an ascending oxer? What kind of combination are you being asked to jump; does it consist of two uprights or is it an upright to an oxer?

Make a mental note of the turns and the distances, and be sure you know the position of the start and the finish. There is nothing more galling than being eliminated for not going through the start or finish, and it is no good coming to a halt as soon as you have landed over the final fence, accruing time faults for not having gone through the finish.

Now that you have walked the course you know exactly where you are going to go and how you are going to ride to each fence. The course is well planned out mentally. Sit down quietly, shut your eyes and ride the course in your head. Do this at least twice. Visualise yourself jumping a beautifully judged, clear round. Either see yourself riding the course as you would on a video or from your riding position on your horse's back, seeing each fence approach through your horse's ears. See and feel the potential problems and deal with each problem as it arises. Familiarise yourself with every eventuality, but especially that beautifully ridden and perfectly timed clear round. Convince yourself that this is the round you are going to achieve. Positive visualisation has great merit.

# CHAPTER 17

# Competition Technique

## In the collecting ring

Now it is time to get on your horse and prepare him for his round.

In ideal circumstances, warm up your horse away from the collecting ring and enter it only when you are ready to jump the practice jump(s). There are usually two practice fences – an upright and an oxer. They will both have a red flag or wing on one side – always keep this **R**ed flag or wing to your **R**ight.

When in the collecting ring, remember to pass other riders left to left, and always overtake on the inside.

When you are riding your horse in, the effect you are trying to achieve is a state of complete tranquillity and harmony between you. You are trying to produce a quietly submissive, supple horse, who is in balance, in rhythm, active and mentally alert. Unfortunately, this is not always possible as other riders and their horses suddenly cut across your track, oblivious to collecting-ring etiquette, i.e. jumping fences 'backwards', cannoning into your horse's quarters and running out just in front of your horse's nose.

Once you are in the warm-up area your horse has to get down to work. You should not slop around for hours on a long rein talking to your friends, nor should you thrash around at the last moment, throwing your horse over half a dozen big fences before dashing into the arena. You must concentrate on working your horse in such a way that when he starts jumping fences he

will jump them well. This may take a little while but if your horse is not paying attention to you when you warm up then you are going to crash and burn when you attempt to jump him.

The practice jump area is a warming-up area – it is not a schooling ground. By the time you have arrived at the show your horse should be prepared to jump anything within his scope. He should not need to jump the practice jump endlessly in order to make him (or you) better or braver.

Work your horse quietly on the flat and have him level both physically and mentally before you jump the practice fence. Once you are ready to jump, start with a small cross-pole or vertical just to loosen him up a bit, and then raise the fence steadily. Within half a dozen jumps you should have reached the height you will be jumping in the arena. Now you can attempt an oxer – again, start quite low, so that your horse gets the idea that nothing is going to frighten him, but build up quite rapidly. Make sure that the oxer is neither too big nor too wide. You are not trying to test your horse or school him in the collecting ring, rather you are asking him to stretch and open out a little. Now give yourself a little time to walk around before jumping another vertical, which may be a couple of centimetres higher than you will jump in the arena.

So often one see riders in the collecting ring jumping fences over and over and over again. I can only imagine that their schooling at home has not been thorough enough and they are still trying to get things right at the show.

Make sure you arrive at the entrance to the arena in good time for your round. There is nothing more disconcerting than to be hustled into the arena by an irate collecting steward who has been calling your name for five minutes. Nor do your fellow competitors want to be held up by your incompetence. On the other hand, do not sit on your horse, blocking the entrance, watching the six or seven horses before you. Looking at other people's rounds is a good idea, but do it on your own, on foot, so that you are not in everyone's way.

Ideally, it is only necessary to start jumping-in when there are about five or six horses before you. This should give you time to jump-in, make sure you are comfortable and give your horse a chance to catch his breath before entering the arena.

## The first round

Once you are in the arena, start recalling the plans you have made in your head. Put your horse into a balanced, rhythmic canter, leading with the correct leg for your first turn, and ride though the start. Ride to each fence as you have planned, using all your corners. This will give you more time to think.

If you have a pole down – **forget about it**. You cannot concentrate on the fences ahead of you if you are trying to analyse what went wrong at the fences behind you.

Once you have gone through the finish, get into the custom of riding a circle, with your horse under control and working well, almost as if you are going to start again. Do not get into the dreadful habit of flying out of the ring or dragging your horse into a sliding halt.

Once you have jumped your round, for better or for worse, do not make a scene. It is hoped that you have jumped a good clear that you feel comfortable with, but if you have not, just get straight off once you are out of the arena and keep calm. There is absolutely no need for the horrible 'spoilt brat' scenes that you occasionally

witness in the collecting ring (or even more inexplicably back in the horse box or stables). Tempers sometimes fly, especially at some of the smaller shows, with young or (worse still) not so young people taking their anger out on their poor horses – raking spurs, pulling out back teeth and/or with unnecessary abuse of the whip. Nor is there any need for you to scream at your parents, friends or coach. What is done is done. Learn from your mistakes, go home and iron your problems out there in a civilised manner. If you cannot control your anger, get off and walk away.

Assuming you are one of the lucky, skilled few, and you have jumped a clear round, you should dismount as soon as you leave the arena, loosen your girths and walk your horse around until he stops blowing. When his breathing settles, you can let him stand and relax. Keep his muscles warm with a rug so that he does not develop cramp. A very important part of a good horseman's programme is to ensure that his horse remains in good condition to come and jump again.

## The jump-off

Firstly, you must define your aims. Are you trying to win the competition, or are you trying to gain experience? If it's experience you want you should focus on increasing the level of activity in your horse and raising your own concentration. Study the course plan before you look at the jumps in the arena. Look for some sensible short turns to encourage you both to move up a gear. There is little point in jumping fences for the sake of it. You should be practising quietly and sensibly with future wins as your goal. Make calculated turns so that your horse becomes more used to being turned short into fences, and increase your tempo a little so that he becomes accustomed to being ridden in a slightly upbeat rhythm.

If you are trying to win the competition you need to study the course in even greater detail to analyse all the possible options, i.e. where tight turns can be risked and strides lengthened. Try to have an edge over the other competitors. Look for something that no one else is likely to see, and take that risk. The great thing about show jumping is that if you try something and it comes off you are a hero for a day. However, if you fail, you may look a bit of a fool – but so what, at least you tried!

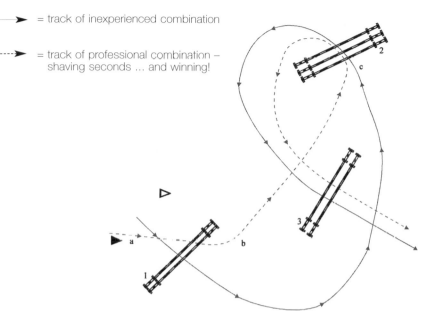

= track of inexperienced combination

= track of professional combination – shaving seconds ... and winning!

**Jump-off technique.**
(a) Coming close to the offside start flag allows the horse to jump the first fence at an angle.
(b) Turning on landing, towards the second fence, allows the horse to cut inside the third fence.
(c) Turning the horse in the air over the second fence allows for a sharp turn to the third fence.

It is easy to see how time and distance can be saved but unless your horse is balanced and well schooled he will be unable to perform such turns. If your horse is stiff and resistant, attempting tight turns will actually waste time as you will be unable to maintain a forward canter stride. You will also run the risk of having refusals, run-outs or knock-downs.

Once again, scrutinise the course first on the written plan and then study the course and jumps in the arena. Make sure you have considered:

- all the tight turns;
- where you can lengthen;
- where you need to shorten;
- how each fence, jumped in a certain way, can lead you on well to the next fence;
- whether you can angle a jump over one fence to get inside another (keep your eye on the gap, never look at the jump you are trying to avoid!); and
- where the start and finish are.

Riding in a jump-off is all about riding wisely with daring, but not recklessly. Remember again, if you are quick-thinking you will have more time to act. Whether you are jumping to gain experience or to win you will need to pick up your jump-off tempo before you go through the start. Do not harbour any doubts or reservations – try to win from the first stride to the last.

## Jump-off techniques

Once you are ready to attack jump-off courses with the intention of winning the class you need to know:

- **how** to turn into fences quickly and from a short distance;
- **how** to turn sharply after fences;
- **how** to jump across fences on an angle; and
- **how** to turn up the tempo.

### TURNING SHORT INTO FENCES

The essential ingredient for turning short into a fence is to be confident and positive about doing so. Primarily you need to practise at home time and time again. To turn short into your fences you need very good balance and a bold attitude. Set up a small fence at home and jump it through a circle. Gradually reduce the size of your circle from approximately 20 to 15 metres, then to 10 metres. Always keep your horse balanced between a strong hand and leg, and encourage him to produce an athletic, rhythmic canter which is one gear up from the speed at which you normally ride. Eventually your horse will become accustomed to meeting the fence off a curve and from a short distance, and to reacting quickly.

Now you can increase the height of the fence and begin to put obstacles in the way of your approach. For instance, you can place a fence wing a few metres in front of the fence and aim to turn inside the wing. Immovable objects around which you will have to manoeuvre your horse are a feature of the competition jump-off, and your ability to move fluently inside these

**Tight turns.** Practise tight turns at home. Here the rider jumps the fence on an angle and starts to turn his horse whilst in the air. Carrying the bend through in a balanced manner, the rider is able to turn his horse inside the wing of another fence. This would save valuable seconds in a jump-off.

obstacles, taking the shortest route from fence to fence, will ultimately affect whether you win a class or become an also-ran.

Never look at the fence or obstacle you are trying to avoid. Once you commit yourself to a turn you must not take your eye off the fence you are about to jump until you are jumping it. If you do, you will either over-shoot it or undershoot it. Your eye will be drawn to the thing that you are trying to avoid – and the chances are that you will ride straight into it! However, if you are trying to ride though a gap, look through the gap.

Once you have committed yourself to a turn do not change your mind. Occasionally, when you have turned the corner and are approaching the fence you will find yourself in a less than perfect place to take off from – do not panic. If you are too far away, keep hold of your horse's head and use plenty of leg; if you are too close, again take a stronger hold on the rein and encourage your horse to create a bigger jump. Always ride with a good amount of leg, indicating to your horse, 'Yes, we are going, and don't worry about a thing.' If you attempt to alter the shape of your curve as you approach the jump you will unbalance your horse and he will arrive to the foot of the jump in a disorganised heap.

Another useful exercise is to construct a right angle with two poles in front of the jump, slightly to one side. Put a cone a couple of metres in from the poles and ride your horse between the cones and the poles as you turn into the jump (see diagram opposite). This will help to improve your balance on the approach to a fence. Alternatively build a right angle in front of the fence with two sets of poles (see photos on facing page).

**Improving balance on the approach to the fence. 03**Using poles placed at right angles to the fence, the rider is able to guide his horse through the corner and towards the canter pole and fence.

## TURNING SHORT AFTER FENCES

Go back to your small, single fence on a 20-metre circle, start to make a change of rein as you jump over the fence. As you take off, look to the opposite rein and encourage your horse to land ready to turn onto the new rein. For example, if you have started your circle on a left bend, look to the right as you take off and turn to the right as you land. Once you have re-established a balanced canter, approach the fence with the intention of turning to the left on landing. Again, look to the left as you take off to encourage your horse to shift his weight onto his left side and to change lead from right to left.

Now you can begin to make a figure-of-eight over

Poles placed like this can help you plan your turn into a jump.

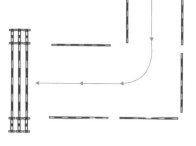

As you practise, you can replace inside poles with a cone so that your turn can be nearer to the jump

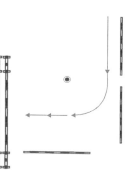

**Figure-of-eight.** Jumping a figure of eight over a fence is a useful exercise to improve turning. You can gradually reduce the diameter of the turning circle to 10m.

your fence (see photo sequence above). Once your horse is happily carrying out this exercise you can gradually reduce the diameter of your circles to 10 metres. When you are trying to turn in the air you not only need to look in the direction in which you intend to turn, but also to make a small adjustment in your weight through your stirrups and to guide your horse onto the new rein with a leading rein. Be warned: too great an adjustment will throw your horse out of balance just as certainly as no adjustment at all, so work on subtlety! To refresh your memory on turning, refer back to 'Basic Work on the Flat' (Chapter 6) and turning over fences on pages 99 and 100.

As a progression from the poles and cone exercise described above, position a pair of poles at a right angle with a central cone after the jump as well as before it, so that you have to perform a balanced turn after you

land as well as before you take off (see diagram opposite). Alternatively, use two sets of poles to make the right-angle channel (see photos on facing page).

## JUMPING ON ANGLES

Jumping on an angle is part of the ammunition that you need for good jump-off results. The fastest way to get between two points is in a straight line. If you can confi-

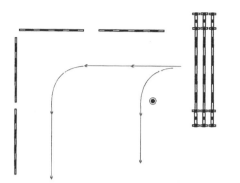

Using poles and a cone to guide your turn after a jump. As you practise you can get closer and closer to the cone.

dently cut across an angle over a jump it can also set you up for a much better turn after the jump. If you are brave enough to ride that straight line even if an angled fence is in the way, you will beat the rider who makes three or more changes of direction to approach that fence in a straight line.

The most common mistake made by riders coming to fences at an angle is to try and turn square to the fence at the very last moment. This shows a lack of confidence – so how do you increase your confidence? Practise at home! To practise jumping on angles you need to give yourself a very clear line to work from. Set up a small, upright fence and place a pole a couple of metres in front of it at the angle at which you want to jump from (position 1); this guide pole will help to line

**Tight turns.** Here the right-angle poles are placed after the jump and are used to guide the horse through the corner after he has landed.

you up for the fence (see diagram below). As you become more confident, increase the angle of the pole (position 2) and eventually remove the pole altogether.

The most common mistake made by horses coming to fences at an angle is that they run out through the outside shoulder. You must insure against this eventuality by a firmness on both reins and a strong outside leg, keeping your horse to the required track. Your priority is to keep the horse channelled between your hands and legs, towards the fence, at the point you want to jump

Using an angled pole in front of a jump (position 1) will teach the horse to jump across a fence. Start by using a vertical and progress to an oxer. The better you get, the more acute you can make your approach (position 2). Remember, though, that the fence becomes much wider when jumped on an angle, so don't be too ambitious.

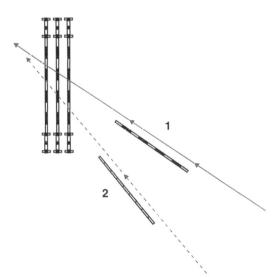

it. The area of the fence that you aim for is exactly the same as if you were approaching it head-on – the middle two feet of the poles or planks. If you keep yourself focused on this area your horse is less likely to be able to run out. Jumping fences at an angle will teach you to be more accurate.

Jumping oxers at an angle is more difficult than jumping upright fences. The width of the spread on such fences is increased if you jump them at an angle, and obviously the width of an oxer is increased to a far greater extent than that of an upright. You must be careful not to frighten yourself or your horse, and you must practise at home before trying to jump an angled oxer in a competition. Build a very small, narrow oxer to start practising over, again using a guide pole, and gradually increase the height and width of the oxer as you both become more confident and capable.

Once you can jump fences on an angle without using the guide pole, you can jump them through a figure-of-eight. Put a guide pole a few metres after the fence as well, training you to maintain your line after jumping (see diagram below left). It is just as important to move away from the fence at the correct angle as it is to approach it from the correct angle. Line up three fences, three or four strides apart, each set at an angle. Use poles to create a channel between the fences and approach the fences from both reins. Progress to jumping double combinations in the same manner using a staggered or offset double (see diagram below). These exercises will improve your angle jumping, your accuracy and your related distance riding – pretty useful really!

Throughout all these exercises you must keep your horse light in his shoulders and powerful in his haunches; you must also enable him to maintain his balance – balance is the key to saving seconds in the jump-off.

Remember that you are riding a straight line from Point A to Point B, it is the fence which is at an angle. When you walk a competition course always keep the jump-off in mind. If you realise that you will want to jump a fence at an angle in the jump-off, walk the angle. Find yourself a Point A and look towards Point B. Look for a noticeable landmark at Point B to aim for. From Point B, look back to Point A and check that the line you have drawn for yourself is a good one. Once you are on your horse in the jump-off, as you approach the fence from Point A keep your eye on that landmark at Point B. This will help you to maintain your straight line and will discourage you from trying to meet the fence straight on.

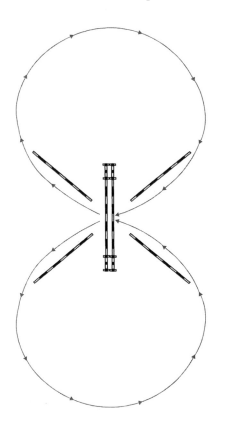

**Jumping a figure-of-eight over a fence at an angle.** This is a progression from the exercise shown in the preceding diagram. Try to encourage your horse to land on the correct leg, but if he doesn't, either bring him back to trot and change to the correct lead or perform a flying change.

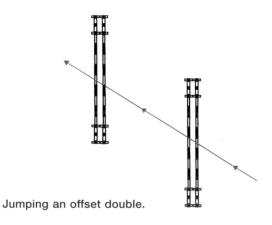

**Jumping an offset double.**

## UPPING THE TEMPO

Galloping over show jumps is not the same as galloping over steeplechase fences or fixed obstacles. You cannot brush through or scrape over show jumps; you have to ensure that all the poles are left up. The bigger the jump, the more difficult it is to clear – particularly at the gallop, which produces a long, flat stride. Therefore we do not gallop at fences, we open our horse up over fences and increase their stride after them. Two or three strides before the fence we return our horse to a 'rubber-ball' canter so that he is ready to take off in a short, balanced stride.

Try to organise your gallop so that you move on for five or ten strides but are able to close your horse up for three or four strides afterwards. This is something you can practise whilst at home, either in the school or out on a hack. As you close your horse up think about getting his hocks underneath him, creating energy. This all harks back to our flatwork and creating an infinite adjustability of the horse's gait. You will never win a jump-off if it takes you seven or eight strides to increase or decrease your tempo. Your horse may need some strong hand and leg aids to begin with to instil in him the idea of instant obedience and tempo change, and the ensuing leaps forward, head throwing and paddling may not be a very pretty sight. However, the sooner he understands what he is being asked to do, the sooner the aids can be refined. The more you practise, the more responsive your horse will become. Ultimately, your horse will be capable of making quite radical changes of pace within one or two strides.

# CHAPTER 18

# *What Happens If ...?*

This chapter looks at some of the common problems experienced at competitions and offers advice on the best course of action. Suggestions on how to deal with ridden problems (such as rushing, rearing, bucking, napping, etc.) and stable vices (kicking, biting, weaving, etc.) are given in Chapter 22.

**"WHAT HAPPENS IF I ARRIVE LATE AT A SHOW?"**
If you arrive late, for whatever reason – e.g. your horse would not load, you got lost, broke down or ran out of diesel – firstly, do not panic, scream and flap. Panic only ever makes things worse.

If you do miss the class – well, it is just one class, not the end of civilisation as we know it; but the chances are that if you stay calm, get your horse and yourself kitted up, and get down to the arena in the quickest time you can, without flustering your horse, you will not miss your class. Note the emphasis put on not flustering your horse: he does not know that you are late, so the best thing to do is not to upset him.

Given that you arrive at the collecting ring and there are only a couple of horses left to go in the class, or they are already calling for you, just canter around the collecting ring for a few minutes, calmly and in good balance – do not jump the practice fence.

You will not have a chance to walk the course so you will not be aware of the distances between fences, but you should have seen one horse jump the course and

hopefully someone will have given you some idea of the route. As you enter the arena give the course a quick scan before embarking on your round, but remember that once the bell has gone you must begin your round within 30 seconds.

Once that bell has gone you are no longer late, you are in exactly the same place now as you would have been if you had arrived two hours ago – so make the most of it. You must jump your round at exactly the same speed and in exactly the same rhythm as you would have done if you had had hours of preparation.

Generally, the first three fences on a course are not too difficult so treat those as warm-up fences. Make sure that you ride them as accurately and as correctly as you can. Now you have the confidence to start your round at fence four and to jump to the best of your ability.

Had you got in a flap, crashed around a few practice fences, flown into the arena and commenced your round in a state of tension and confusion, your horse would have become distressed, tense and totally unbalanced. You would have started jumping in a bad manner, your round would have been awful and you would have been sure that your day would not improve as it went on.

**"WHAT IF MY WARM-UP GOES BADLY?"**
You have arrived in plenty of time, you are totally organised, you arrive at the practice area and ... you find

the going bears a resemblance to concrete, or it is hock-deep in mud, or there are thirty horses cannoning into each other in an area the size of a postage stamp and you cannot give your horse a correct nor sufficient warm-up.

To begin with, get out of the warm-up area. Relax and walk around the showground in permitted areas. Compose yourself and try to think of an alternative plan. This is going to involve loosening up your horse as much as you can in walk. You can now use all your 'More Advanced Work on the Flat' skills (see Chapter 7). Exercises using shoulder-in, leg-yielding and rein-back are all going to help loosen up your horse in a better way than will standing around fretting or trying

to dart in and out of a mêlée of other horses.

If there is a lull in the practice arena you may be able to slip in and carry out a small amount of trot and canter work. If the going in the practice area is just impossible to jump on, you should resort to using the first three jumps in the arena as your warm-up jumps (as above), praying that the going in the arena itself is better than that outside it. Your horse is correctly trained and you are jumping within your comfort zone so you will cope.

There are few things worse than trying to warm up in very poor conditions. Each horse in the competition will jump the fences in the competition only once, but they will jump the practice fence six or seven times (at least!), so imagine how bad the going is likely to get! Seriously deep and holding ground will not only tire your horse, but also will cause your horse a loss of

**Horses are great levellers.** Despite meticulous preparation, things can and do go wrong.

confidence and may lead to strain and injury of joints, tendons and ligaments.

When you enter the arena check the going in front of the fences. Most horses will have aimed, correctly of course, for the middle two feet of the fence, so the ground towards the centre of the fence is likely to be badly cut up. However, the going five feet either side, towards the wings, should be much better. Because you are riding an impeccably schooled horse, you can aim him closer to the wings of the fences without fear of him running out! (Obviously there will be other riders in the competition who have read this book, so you will not be treading on virgin turf, but you should definitely find better going either side of the centre of the fence.)

## "WHAT IF I HAVE DONE EVERYTHING RIGHT YET I STILL JUMPED A BAD ROUND?"

A poor round could range from having one refusal or a pole down, to skittling poles down left, right and centre, or being eliminated for three refusals or a fall. It could even mean that you have jumped clear but felt that you did not deserve to because you were riding badly or that your horse was misbehaving.

If you jumped clear but felt that you rode badly, put the round behind you, think positively and resolve to do better in the next round. If your horse behaved badly because he was too fresh, work him! After you leave the arena walk him around for a few minutes to allow him to catch his breath, and then work him. Do not jump him over a thousand fences, but work him on the flat. The difficulty is to keep your adrenaline under control and not to become tense due to competition nerves. Walk, trot and canter him just as you would at home. Give him something to think about such as frequent transitions, leg-yielding and rein-back. Once you have worked the edge off his freshness, walk him for a little while then let him stand and cool off before you begin warming up for the jump-off.

If your horse has scattered poles to the four winds, the first thing to remember is to keep your temper under control. You cannot turn back the clock and have your round again, so accept defeat graciously. Now analyse why you had fences down. Rushed preparation, bad riding, poor warm-up facilities or an over-fresh horse should be easy reasons to pin down, but if none of these was apparently at the root of the problem you

**John Whitaker**

"The more you practise the better you will be, but you will always be learning from your mistakes. Sit down and think about what you did wrong and try to work out how things could have gone better. Should you have gone faster? Should you have tried to get in one more stride between two fences? Once you think you know the answer store that information and remember to use it when a similar situation arises."

must look deeper. Has your horse got a physical problem? Do not seek excuses for him but do trot him up and check whether his gait is normal and if he is totally sound. Does he appear particularly stiff on one rein or another, possibly signifying muscle problems in his back? Does he appear 'under the weather', in which case he may have a virus? If your horse is suddenly off his feed this is a good sign that something is awry and he may need his blood analysed by your veterinarian.

Horses can only use their talent if they are fit and well. A long season can jade your horse's enthusiasm and take its toll on his physical and mental well-being. Because you are with your horse day after day you may miss subtle changes in his appearance. Stand well back and have a good, detached look at him. Is he lean and fit or just too thin; conversely, is he well muscled or just too fat? Is he fit, or is he just overfed and fizzy? If you do not feel that you can be objective ask a knowledgeable friend to assess him.

If he does not appear to have any glaring physical problems think about the basics. Has he had good

*Points to ponder...*

- *Whether you think you can or can't ... you're right!*

preparation and homework leading up to the event? Is he ready to jump the category of class you have entered him in? Have you checked his feet, teeth and tack? The list is endless but the important point to make is that horses do not become clumsy because they choose to be, there is nearly always something wrong if they suddenly start having fences down.

Refusals may come about as a result of any of the above problems, but what many riders fail to recognise is that often the problem is of their own making. Assuming all your preparations have gone to plan and everything else appears fine, perhaps you should ask yourself this question: are you overfacing yourself? This does not imply that you are chicken, or that you should doubt your own ability; in fact, the whole problem of overfacing yourself may stem from too much bravado and a desire to prove to the world that you are better than you are.

For instance, suppose you have bought a good, experienced horse that has won 4ft 3ins (1.30m) classes. Your ego may push you to try and enter 4ft 3ins (1.30m) classes when you may only be confident and proficient in 3ft 9ins (1.10m) classes. This particular problem is witnessed most often when pony riders are pushed by over-enthusiastic parents, when pony riders make the step up to horses, or when riders come to the sport at a mature age and think it all looks rather simple.

Sadly, very few horses are 'jumping machines'. Confidence, as I have said all along, is fragile: it takes years to build and seconds to shatter. Show jumping is a partnership and even the best horse needs an adequate partner. Imagine putting £1 into the till every time you jump well and taking £5 out every time you jump badly – if you keep overfacing yourself, you will become bankrupt remarkably quickly!

Top international riders jumping 5ft 3ins (1.60m) classes have a wealth of experience and confidence behind them. They are riding horses that are more than capable of jumping 5ft 6ins (1.70m), and at home they will occasionally be asked to do so. These riders are entering the ring knowing that they can call on well-honed skills and an extra 3–4ins (10cm) of height and scope if they need it. When you buy your schoolmaster, ride him at a height you feel confident with so that you can call on his extra experience and those extra few centimetres if you need them.

If your horse is young and you are frightened of spoiling him, the rules are very similar. Try to avoid situations which are likely to invite refusals. Prevention is better than cure. Most horses gain confidence by not being hurt, by doing things well and by receiving praise when they do so. This is how a bold, confident horse is created. If a young horse believes that he will hurt himself once he enters the arena, he will soon start to refuse to jump.

If you have been eliminated for having refusals and you know that the most probable cause is overfacing, do not be too proud to enter a smaller class at the next show you go to. Even if you have to jump *hors concours* in a novice class, most shows will be more than happy to accommodate you. They may even allow you to jump *hors concours* in the jump-off.

### "WHAT IF I HAVE A FALL?"

Unfortunately, occasionally you will have a fall. Current BSJA and FEI rules state that if you fall off you are eliminated and you must leave the arena. Obviously, if you or your horse is injured in the fall you should not attempt to jump again in the collecting ring. If you are not injured it would seem sensible to attempt to regain your horse's confidence straight away.

Having ascertained that your horse has not injured himself in any way, you can take him into the collecting ring and jump four or five fences to renew his confi-

**Michel Robert**

❝ Always look for the problem in the mind of the rider, not in the body of the horse. Always look for the solution in the mind of the rider and not in the body of the horse.

Take care of the basics and establish them well; overlooking the simple things will always catch up with you and cause difficulties. ❞

dence. Keep the fences low and narrow to start with, but before you finish try to raise them to a height comparable to the fence at which you fell. If you can enter another, similar height class in the same arena, so much the better. The fall may have been apparently innocuous, but horses do remember falls for a long time, particularly if they have hurt themselves, and if the fall frightened you, you can rest assured that it frightened your horse even more.

## "AT THE END OF THE DAY ..."

If you are riding your own horse at a show the most important thing to remember is that you are not there to please your parents, your groom or your coach – you are there to please yourself.

Whether you have won or lost at the end of the day, you will need to hold a brief review of your round(s). Have you achieved your goal? Have you improved your performance? If problems occurred, do you know why they occurred and do you think you can prevent them from happening again?

Analyse your shortcomings but remember that everybody is human and makes mistakes. Horses are horses and we cannot predict their every move, nor should we get aggravated with them just because they have a bad day. There is always another day and another show. If you are lucky enough to have won the competition remember it is not you who has won, but you and your team. Thank your horse, your groom, your friends, your family and your coach. Also remember to thank the organisers including the judges and the collecting-ring steward. A little courtesy goes a long way!

Again, if something does go wrong at a show it is important not to abandon your system and start to alter all your plans, but if you can detect flaws in the plans you have made and can think of ways of improving them in the future, you have made a positive step to improving your skill. However, if you have been doing the same things for a period of time and the system is definitely not working, look at the whole thing objectively and see what you need to change, or get some fresh advice.

# CHAPTER 19

# Towards Advanced Classes

Your horse's rhythm, impulsion, tempo and balance are now well established; he is familiar with jumping in first-round and jump-off situations, on all terrains and in all weathers at novice level; now he is ready to move on to bigger and better things.

## Higher and wider

What is it that makes it more difficult to achieve success over bigger and wider fences? The one thing that puts most people off tackling the bigger competitions is their own perceived lack of ability. Most riders have more ability than they think they have, and often horses have less ability than their owners think.

Not every horse that is sold as a show jumper is going to be capable of jumping enormous tracks, yet most people who go out and buy such a horse believe that they can. The realisation that a horse is not going to become an internationally renowned Grand Prix star can be painful for both owner and horse.

A horse that is constantly faced with jumps that are at the limit of, or even beyond, his scope will become frightened, sore and resentful. Eventually he will throw in the towel and will refuse habitually, nap, or even refrain from entering the arena at all. Yet if the same horse is allowed to continue jumping at a height that he feels comfortable with, he should give somebody years of pleasure as a schoolmaster. There is no tangible way of knowing how high your horse can jump other than stepping into the unknown, gradually introducing him to bigger and bigger courses. Only you will be able to tell whether or not your horse is comfortable and capable of answering these bigger questions.

Throughout your horse's training you should gradually introduce (firstly) wider and (then) higher fences. You can easily introduce wider fences coming out of a combination, within a grid or at the end of a related distance. It is important that you do not ask your horse to lengthen his stride when coming into the wider fence. Instead you need to shorten his stride slightly. This will give you an indication of whether your horse is confident enough to open out and jump the wider fences. I prefer to use a double with a one-, two- or three-stride distance, with the oxer as the second element, to test the horse and to encourage him to open himself out over the fence.

Once you have ascertained that your horse is capable of jumping a wider fence, you need to find out whether he can also jump higher. Using the same combination, grid or related stride as before, close the oxer right up, perhaps to just a 1ft (30cm) spread, lower the front rail and raise the back rail higher than you would normally; for example, if you are comfortable at jumping 3ft 7½ins (1.10m), then raise the back rail to 3ft 11ins (1.20m) or even 4ft 3ins (1.30m).

Do not raise any fence more than 2ins (5cm) at a time; this way the fence does not become too daunting too quickly. Always try to ensure that you have a friend or assistant on the ground when you are widening or increasing the height of fences so that fluency is maintained. In any one session you could raise the fences by 2ins (5cm) up to seven times. Your most important task is to keep meeting these fences at exactly the same pace, in exactly the same rhythm, absorbing the increase in height. This exercise will test your powers of self-control more than it tests your horse. Inevitably, if you are inexperienced, it is you who will run out of courage and confidence before the horse. As soon as you see the fence getting high you will begin to think, 'Gallop'... as soon as you start to think 'Gallop', your horse will run onto his forehand ... and as soon as your horse runs onto his forehand you have lost the battle for control. Think **power**, not speed.

Keeping within the discipline of the double combination or the related distance, you will not meet the second element on a bad stride – given that you have approached the first element on a good stride! Make sure that the fence going in to the combination is not so big that it causes stress to you or your horse, nor so small that it does not prepare your horse for what is to come. Your 'placing fence' should allow you to glide to the second, more testing, fence.

Do not work at increasing height and width at the same time; to do so is more likely to cause problems than to find answers. Once you have ascertained that your horse is capable of jumping wider and higher fences, you can begin to fit these fences into your training courses at home. One note of caution. Do not be in a hurry to prove your horse's new-found abilities at a show. Having jumped good double clears in the beginner and novice classes, do not suddenly be tempted try the Intermediate or Advanced classes.

I am a great believer in the idea that your horse should be able to jump 4ins (10cm) higher at home, on a regular basis, than he needs to jump in the ring, particularly at the novice levels. Obviously once you get above the novice levels, and your horse is jumping well at home, then the amount of jumping you do at home will be reduced, not increased. As long as he is comfortably jumping, at home, the height and width that he will be expected to clear in any jump-off situation, you should feel that you are doing enough.

Always make sure that it is the second element of any

**A dike fence.** A small dike in a practice area.

related distance that is the bigger of the two fences. If you were to make the first element of a related distance the larger, then any mistake you make at that fence will be magnified by the time you reach the second obstacle, leading to BIG problems!

To jump bigger fences you will need more power, not more speed. Once you have developed the skill of creating power in your horse's stride, by keeping him contained between the hand and leg aids, then you can begin to cope with bigger fences. However, remember that the speed at which you approach upright fences will not be the same speed at which you approach spread fences. You need a little more power and speed as you approach spread fences, and you need more accuracy as you approach upright fences. At no time must you gallop flat out at fences, but you must learn to ride at a slightly faster, stronger pace; in fact, you will be expected to do so all the time once you begin to enter the upper-grade competitions.

As you enter the Intermediate stage of show jumping you will start to face treble combinations. Do not put your horse off by trying to jump huge treble combinations at home, but keep them low so that he maintains his confidence when he meets trebles in the ring. The last thing that you want is a horse that is frightened and seeking ways to avoid jumping.

# Derby fences

Assuming you have accustomed your horse to ditches, banks and water fences, it is time to put him to the test in the arena. This will be quite daunting initially, but we are fortunate that today most outdoor show centres offer novice Derbys, in which the obstacles are quite small and straightforward. As you progress you will come across different obstacles, but most of them will follow a certain formula:

### THE DEVIL'S DIKE

Probably the most famous of all the Derby fences and certainly the most tricky – it requires a bold approach. It consists of three vertical fences, usually a stride apart. The ground slopes down from the first fence to the middle fence (which will have a ditch under it), and then upwards to the final fence. A Devil's Dike is often approached too slowly; this gives the horse time to look into the dike and to balk. It needs to be approached on a bold, forward stride out of a strongish canter but with your horse kept well between hand and leg. Ride the last few strides as if you mean to get through, not with a backward-thinking attitude. If your horse is unsure of himself, the last thing he needs is for you to feel unsure too.

At the beginning you will have to risk the chance of dropping a pole at the first fence for the sake of getting all the way through, but I am definitely not advocating the idea of galloping blindly ahead. What I am saying is that you must gather up your horse's impulsion between your hand and leg and drive him strongly towards the dike, not allowing him to become flat and loose.

You must ride your horse just as boldly through the second and third elements as you did to the first. Remember that because of the upwards slope, the 'out' fence is going to be bigger than the fence coming in, and the distance to the fence will seem longer for the same reason.

Do not worry about the slope going down to the middle fence – that is not a 'horse' problem, it is a perceived 'rider' problem. Your horse's momentum will carry him down perfectly to the second element, as long as you have driven him well into the first – but he may balk at the ditch so keep his head up and keep your legs on.

A big dike combination.

### THE WATER JUMP

These are designed to test your horse's ability to jump width and his boldness to jump over water. Contrary to public opinion, you do not have to gallop flat out at a water jump to clear it! Nor do you need to canter to it too slowly. And whatever you do, do not try to find a perfect stride from which to take off.

Get your horse into a good, balanced, forward-thinking stride, held completely between your hands and your legs, and then do not hesitate. Whatever you feel, keep going and ninety times out of hundred you will arrive at the fence in an acceptable place to take off from. My theory is that my horse needs to get to the fence a fraction before I do. If I am (just) a split second behind him, I am less likely to get an early bath. (Like most people, I have had one or two of those. There is nothing more uncomfortable than getting back into the saddle with soggy breeches and swilling boots.)

The easiest way of getting your horse over water jumps in the arena is to have made sure that he is fully at ease with getting over them at home. It is also important that your horse is quite comfortable in and around

Water. The first type of water fence you are likely to encounter in a competition

Water. The biggest type of water fence you are ever likely to meet. Note the height the horse has gained.

water. At one time, show jumpers were loath even to get their horses' feet wet in case it taught them bad habits, e.g. they would not try their hardest to clear the whole jump. I prefer my horses to understand that water will not harm them. I will happily ride them through puddles, streams and ponds, and even into the sea, increasing their knowledge and decreasing their fears. It is easy to ride to a water jump when your horse is taking you there willingly, but virtually impossible if he is not. Most horses that refuse to jump water have been frightened by it at some time.

### A DOUBLE OF WATER DITCHES OR A DOUBLE OF DRY DITCHES

This is really another step in the water-jump saga. If your horse is confident jumping over water and is happy jumping double or treble combinations, then a pair of water ditches should cause you no anxieties or problems. You should be able to ride confidently to the ditches, just as you would to ordinary double combinations.

Set up your canter and remember to be a fraction of a second behind your horse; also remember to keep a

An open ditch. Introduce your horse to an open ditch just as you would to a water tray – see page 83.

Bank fence. An inviting, gentle gradient. The first type of bank you are likely to meet.

**The famous Derby bank at Hickstead.**

good contact on your horse's head as you approach the ditches. If you get in front of your horse's movement, or allow him to drop his head to peer into the ditches, you are likely to be deposited at your horse's feet, probably coming to rest in the ditch itself!

## THE DERBY BANK

Derby banks come in all shapes and sizes – the ultimate Derby bank is the one we have all seen on television, the Derby bank built by Douglas Bunn and used in the Hickstead Derby at The All–England Show Jumping Course. I rather suspect that not many of you will ever experience the thrill of travelling down the steep face of that bank. Even to stand at the edge of it and look down is quite daunting, and the first trip down it is somewhat frightening!

However, you will almost certainly come up against some type of bank in your jumping career, but most will be quite shallow. Banks are not there to be crawled down, but to be ridden down strongly. Riding downhill is easier than most people think. Horses, generally speaking, do not fall head over heels as soon as they encounter a downwards slope – they will balance themselves beautifully as long as their rider keeps still and does not interfere with them. Remember that your horse's balance is not static, it is dynamic – and your job is to sit at the centre of your horse's balance so that you do not cause him to become unbalanced.

When your horse travels downhill, you should let your shoulders come forward, allowing your weight to move slightly forwards, thus keeping your weight in the middle of your horse and off his quarters. This does not mean that you have to get in front of the horse's movement, because you keep your leg in a strong, forward position. If you allow your lower leg to slip backwards then you **will** put too much weight on your horse's shoulder, you **will** get ahead of his action, and you **will**

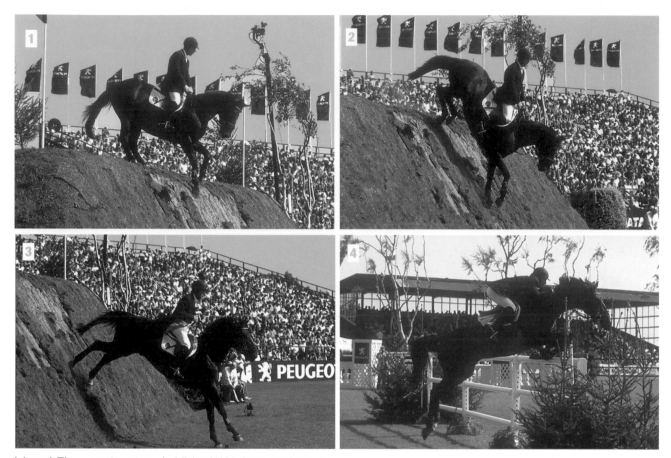

(above) **The maestro at work.** Michael Whitaker negotiates the bank and rail in the 1999 Hickstead Derby. A rail down in the Devil's Dike denied Michael his fourth victory.

(below) **A less conventional trip down the bank.** Although the combination appear to have made a good start, the horse has been a little too exuberant, with an uncomfortable result for him and his jockey.

lose your balance – probably causing your horse to lose his – and you will almost certainly reach the bottom of the slope before your horse!

If there is a fence at the bottom of the bank then you will need to be travelling at the right speed to jump it – you will have to meet it in a balanced canter. Your horse will already be well onto his hocks having come down the bank, and will be ready to jump. If you are cantering downhill you will find, amazingly, that your horse will maintain his own rhythm. You would be hard

pushed to make any horse go quicker running downhill – even the fizziest horse will slow himself down to a sensible rate when travelling downhill.

As long as you can balance yourself and balance your horse, you can canter down the steepest slope. Many years ago the Italian cavalry, the Tore de Quinto, used to carry out an exercise in which a whole troop would canter their horses down what appeared to be an almost vertical slope in a classical, Caprilli seat – anyone who fell off probably had to muck out the whole stables for a year, yet they were unlikely to come off because no horse will ever go faster downhill than it wants to!

**The Derby bank claims another victim.** By coming down the bank sideways and out of balance, this horse is unable to regain his balance before the rails, leading to a refusal.

## ROAD CROSSINGS OR TABLE FENCES

These do not usually cause too much of a problem; again, what you must remember is to approach them boldly. If you jump onto them boldly and jump off them boldly you should have no difficulties. Do not worry about how you land – the drop is no greater than when jumping an ordinary fence of the same height. In other words, if the height of the crossing is 3ft 3ins (1m)

A road crossing or table fence.

**Tackling a road crossing or table fence.** Jumping onto and off a crossing/table.

and the drop is 4ft 3ins (1.30m) then it is no different from jumping a fence that is 4ft 3ins (1.30m) high, so do not let the drop trouble you. If there is a ditch in front of or behind the crossing you must approach the crossing with the same attitude as when approaching a ditch before or after an ordinary fence – boldly and in balance.

# CHAPTER 20

# Saddlery and Tack

Training your horse correctly involves working him in the equipment that suits him best. A simple snaffle bit and a cavesson noseband may not be the answer. If your horse has a delicate mouth, for example, he may not like the nutcracker action of the snaffle and may work better in a straight-mouthed bit. It is your responsibility and that of your coach to ensure that you equip your horse for comfort and control.

A word of advice: whatever you use on your horse make sure that it fits well and that your bridle, saddle-cloth, pad or numnah and girth are kept free from sweat and dirt. Make a point of brushing or washing the sweat from your horse's saddle patch and bridle track each time you ride. Sweat galls are one of the most common reasons for the fit horse being out of work but can be avoided with a little care.

## Saddles

Ninety per cent of today's show jumpers are sitting in modern, close-contact saddles, which are very comfortable, but there are still some riders who prefer the older style of jumping saddle, with their deeper panels, larger saddle flaps and more pronounced knee and thigh rolls (see photos overleaf). My advice on saddles is merely this: make sure the saddle fits your horse, allowing him freedom to move and to jump. And as long as you are both comfortable, you can use whatever saddle you like.

## Nosebands

The type of noseband you use should depend entirely on your horse. In a perfect world the well-schooled horse would never try to open his mouth, cock his jaw or attempt to get his tongue over the bit – but the world is not perfect and they do!

I use only three types of noseband: the cavesson, the cavesson noseband with a flash attachment, and the Grakle. I like to use thick and padded nosebands. Thin leather nosebands can cause pressure and discomfort and a horse that does not feel comfortable will not listen to his rider.

The cavesson noseband is designed to prevent the horse from opening his mouth, but some horses manage to do so and therefore evade the instruction of the bit. On these horses I will use the flash, which is a strap attached to the front of the noseband and fitted under the horse's chin below the bit. I do not believe in fastening the flash too tightly, and still like to be able to slip a finger between the flash and the horse's nose.

> ### Points to ponder...
> - Buy a saddle you can ride in; buy a horse you can ride.

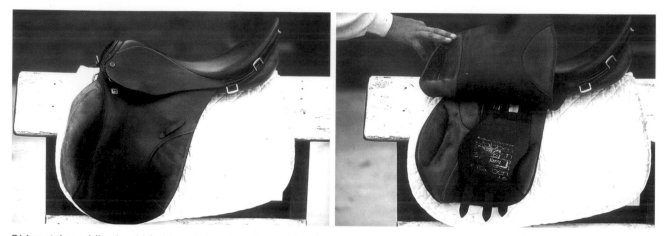

**Older-style saddle.** An old-fashioned show-jumping saddle, showing a deep seat and a high cantle. Lifting the flap reveals copious amounts of padding.

**A modern jumping saddle.** Note the flatter, 'close-contact' seat. The modern saddles have far less padding than earlier designs.

A well-fitted snaffle bridle.  A well-fitted double bridle.  A well-fitted Hackamore.

In my view, drop nosebands never seem to work – not because the theory behind them is flawed but because they just do not seem to be made correctly. All too often the padded upper band is too short, and the length of narrow, unpadded straps which loop under the bit and the chin, are too long. Thus the pressure on the sides of the horse's jowls is concentrated on too narrow an area, leading to soreness. Also the buckle invariably fastens just by the bars of the bit, which means there is a mass of ironwork just waiting to trap the tender sides of the horse's mouth.

Grakles are usually effective against horses that evade the bit by opening the mouth or by crossing their jaw. I like to ensure that they are fitted high enough, and for that reason prefer the Mexican Grakle to the old-fashioned English Grakle.

## Bitting

Again, in the ideal world every horse would have a mouth like velvet and we would all be riding in single-jointed, loose-ring snaffles – but every horse is different. It used to be thought that thick-barred bits were kindest and the most mild, but recent research shows that the area of the mouth in which the bit sits is not as wide as was previously thought.

Horses do get strong, and if they get so strong that you have to start hauling them about, it is probably kinder to put a different bit in their mouth. I would

*Points to ponder...*

- *There is a mouth at the end of the reins.*

usually progress along the lines of:

(a) a thinner barred bit such as a sweet iron, possibly with large rings;
(b) a double-jointed bit such as a KK training bit or a French link;
(c) a correction bit which has an extra loop at the bottom for the rein attachment;
(d) a mullen-mouthed or straight-barred bit;
(e) a vulcanite pelham;
(f) a double bridle;
(g) an American gag.

Before resorting to bits that employ a curb action (i.e. the pelhams and the double bridle) I might also look at alternative types of snaffle, such as the cherry roller, the copper roller, the Waterford, or a plain gag with two reins.

I would not consider using a Dr Bristol. In my opinion this bit should be banned – it is like putting a razor blade in the horse's mouth!

If your horse is able to put his tongue over the bit you will have less control as he has negated the bit's action. There are several devices that deter him from putting his tongue over the bit – e.g. port-mouth snaffles, the

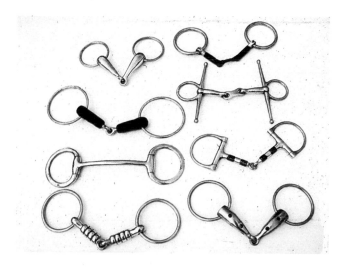

**Bits.** A selection of snaffle bits.

**Bits.** A selection of stronger bits.

**How to measure and fit a standing martingale**

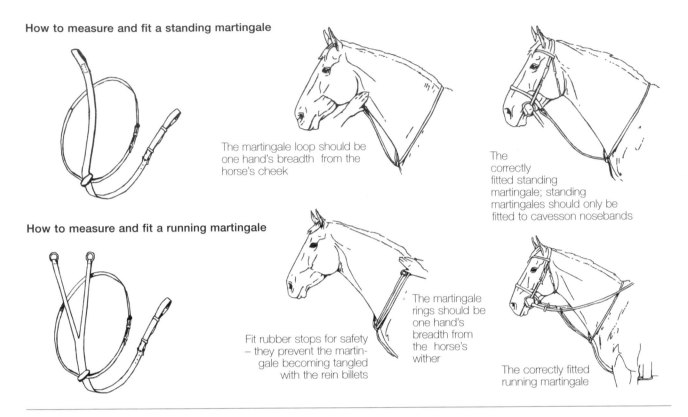

The martingale loop should be one hand's breadth from the horse's cheek

The correctly fitted standing martingale; standing martingales should only be fitted to cavesson nosebands

**How to measure and fit a running martingale**

Fit rubber stops for safety – they prevent the martingale becoming tangled with the rein billets

The martingale rings should be one hand's breadth from the horse's wither

The correctly fitted running martingale

Australian cheeker (or noseband), and rubber tongue ports. Or you could try using a flash attachment or a Grakle and shortening the cheek pieces by one or even two holes on either side, thus lifting the bit in the horse's mouth. If necessary, you may need to employ all three methods.

If your horse has a problem with his mouth, be it medical or mental, then the Blairs pattern bitless bridle or (as it is very frequently but incorrectly called) Hackamore will be invaluable to you; it may also be useful if your horse is just too strong in any other type of bit. Pressure from the reins results in pressure on the poll, nose and lower jaw and, if the cheeks are long, that pressure can be severe.

The bitless bridle should be used only by riders who have already achieved a very strong and independent seat so that the horse's head will not be interfered with whilst jumping. Because its action can be severe I believe it should not be used by children or novice riders.

Although the bitless bridle will help you to stop your horse it will not help with steering, which can be a real drawback in a situation involving tight or short turns.

## Reins

I prefer to use wide, rubber reins – rubber, so that they do not slip in the rain, and wide, because they tend to stay in the hand better, even with a lighter grip. However, if I am using reins in conjunction with draw reins I would rather have a thinner set of reins as my hands become too full.

I also like Continental webbing reins with leather stops. They also give good grip in the wet and they can help the more novice rider to keep an even contact on both reins.

I am not keen on plaited reins, and plain leather reins are purely for the showing ring, not the jumping arena.

I nearly always wear gloves when riding. My own are deer hide roper's gloves, but any type of riding gloves will help you to grip the reins more effectively.

## Martingales

Martingales, if fitted correctly, can be a great help in the arena. Unfortunately, incorrectly fitted martingales, restricting the horse's action to a point that he is unable to jump or move correctly or effectively, are seen all too often. Martingales should prevent the horse from getting his head above the point of control – they should not tie his head down in a fixed position. In time, the horse will learn to set himself against any badly fitting martingale and will become stiff and hollow.

### THE STANDING MARTINGALE

This device runs from the girth, through a neck strap and attaches to a cavesson noseband. There has, for many years, been a rumbling debate as to whether standing martingales should be permitted in the show jumping ring. There should be no problem about using a standing martingale in the arena, provided it is not so tight that it interferes with the horse's shape over the jump. It is a very useful, humane aid that does not inhibit the way the horse jumps as long as it is fitted correctly.

When correctly fitted you should be able to lift the martingale strap into the horse's gullet when he is holding his head in a correct position (shown left). You should be able to place a vertical hand between the neckstrap and your horse's wither. In this position the standing martingale will not have any effect on the horse unless he tries to throw his head up beyond the point of control. The standing martingale, when used and fitted correctly, will help the green, unschooled horse to maintain a more constant head carriage, and will act as a steadier pair of hands for the less experienced rider.

### THE RUNNING MARTINGALE

This runs from the girth to a neck strap (fitted as shown left), at which point it divides and is then attached by two rings to each rein. Rubber or leather rein stops must be used to prevent the martingale rings becoming ensnared with the bit end of the reins (although this is less likely to happen using the more modern, loop-ended reins).

If fitted correctly, with the two rings being able to reach the horse's crest, the running martingale will have no effect on the horse until he throws his head up beyond the point of control. Yet, as with the standing martingale, it is all too often fitted too tightly and pulls down on the bars of the horse's mouth, causing discomfort and a bad jumping style.

## Schooling aids and gadgets

I do not have a problem with people using training aids and auxiliary reins; what I do have a problem with is people using those aids or reins when they not skilled enough to do so properly. This can be foolish if not downright cruel. Schooling aids in the wrong hands are a bit like a cut-throat razor in the hands of a monkey. I have often thought that the people most qualified to use schooling aids are those least likely to do so.

During my career with horses I have used nearly every training aid in the book. Most I have discarded almost immediately, some I have used to advantage for periods of time, and a few I have used to great advantage over a number of years. The two fundamental points to remember are:

- does the horse actually need the aid?
- does the rider understand the aid's function and use?

Training aids should not be used on very young horses. Young horses should be allowed to develop their musculature, balance and strength in a natural way. Using artificial aids on a horse that is not ready, either physically or mentally, is asking for trouble in the long term. Another important point to remember is that unless your horse is moving with impulsion and away from your leg the use of any additional rein or artificial aid is totally futile.

Before you ride or lunge your horse in any form of artificial aid you should ask yourself the following questions.

- Are you experienced enough to cope if something goes wrong?
- Have you studied your horse's temperament and considered whether he is going to be able to cope with the pressures he is about to meet?
- What is his conformation like? Can he physically do what is required?
- Is he fit, or are you going to over-stress him in a serious way by trying to force issues that should be left until he is fit?
- Have you taken good advice from somebody who really knows how these things work?
- Can you do the same job without the use of the aid you are intending to employ?
- Are your skills great enough that you can carry on the

work of the aid once you have removed it?
• Do you really need to use an artificial aid?
• Now that you have answered all the questions above, have you been honest with yourself?

The final point to remember is that no training aid is there to force a horse into a particular shape: it is there to develop that shape. If you have been to a gymnasium to try and develop your own muscles you will know that this takes time. If you force yourself to work too hard for too long you end up with pulled muscles and strained ligaments – in other words a lot of pain for no gain! It is seldom necessary to use any aid for longer than thirty minutes at a time.

## SIDE-REINS AND THE HARBRIDGE

Side-reins are two adjustable reins that usually have either a short elasticated section or a rubber ring inserted along each length to allow some measure of 'give' within the rein itself. They are attached at one end to the rings of the bit, and to the girth, under the saddle flaps, at the other. They are used to keep the horse's head in a correct position whilst on the lunge.

Initially you should fit them so that whilst the horse is relaxed they are taut but are not pulling his head in towards his body. There is no quick-release mechanism for either side-reins or the Harbridge (see below), and if the horse takes a dislike to them there is a fair chance that he may career backwards at speed or rear up, so be careful. Once the horse is used to feeling the action of

the reins they can gradually be tightened until the horse's nose is in a vertical line with his ears. It is the job of the person lungeing the horse to ensure that the horse moves forward into the side-reins and does not tuck his head in to avoid their action or lean heavily on the rein. If not used correctly side-reins will produce a horse that is stiff and backward thinking. (Photo 3.23.1)

Show jumpers often use the side-reins attached to the girth under the horse's belly between his front legs. This type of side-rein is nowadays known as the Harbridge and is used to encourage the horse to maintain a lower head carriage than in side-reins. Again, used correctly it can have some beneficial effect on the way some horses carry themselves.

Side-reins or the Harbridge can be used whilst the horse is being ridden but only by experienced professionals who have a good understanding and feel for the horse they are working with. With every schooling aid there is a possibility of an adverse reaction from the horse, so you must proceed with caution.

## DRAW REINS AND RUNNING REINS

'Just chuck 'im in draw reins – that'll pull 'is 'ead in!' This is a sentence that I hate to overhear but one that is uttered all too frequently. Draw reins are not intended to pull the horse's head in. Their purpose is to encourage the horse to carry his head and neck in a low, flexed manner, in which he can engage his quarters and work through his body. Draw reins will encourage correct

Side reins.

Draw reins.

development and musculature but should not be used on young horses as a matter of course.

The draw rein should only be used when all attempts to create a correct shape have failed. They are a useful aid in the re-schooling of horses that have developed bad habits, such as the horse that is running through the bridle with his jaw crossed and his head in the air. A few sessions in draw reins will put this horse back on the right road and will give him an idea of what is expected. The draw rein is also useful for the horse that refuses to flex through the wither and the poll. It will assist the flexion by encouraging the horse to lower his head and neck onto a longer rein, but you must be careful not to force things. If a horse has been carrying himself in a particular way for a long time then you cannot instantly ask him to carry himself in a different way altogether.

Draw reins can be fitted in two ways; They can either be attached to the girth between the horse's legs, or to the girth straps under the rider's knees. They then pass through the bit and go straight to the rider's hands. Using the latter method, the reins are better known as running reins. The show jumper usually prefers to work with the draw rein, as the jumping horse needs to work in a lower outline than does a dressage horse. The show jumper's aim is to develop the muscles the horse uses to jump, so it makes sense to work in that shape; but in some circumstances it might be a good idea to start working in running reins before progressing to draw

Running reins.

reins. Running reins do not ask the horse to lower his carriage as much as draw reins, so the transition from incorrect to correct head carriage can be gradual.

When the draw rein is being used correctly the rein should be loose once the horse has accepted its pressure, which is achieved through being ridden into it with the rider's leg. When the horse becomes flexible and submissive, the draw rein has no further use and becomes a preventative aid rather than an active aid. Only when the horse raises his head beyond the point of control will the action of the rein come into force again.

Running reins have a similar effect to draw reins but the horse's head will be carried slightly higher. Working a horse in running reins over a long period of time is likely to have a slight fixing effect on the horse's neck, and in time he will find it easy to duck behind the rein and not go forward so well.

## THE MARKET HARBOROUGH AND THE ABBOT DAVIES BALANCING REIN

Several reins have developed directly from the running or draw reins. Two that spring instantly to mind are the Market Harborough and the Abbot Davies Balancing Rein (both shown overleaf).

The action of the **Market Harborough** is similar to that of the draw rein. The reins run between the horse's legs and through the bit rings, but then attach to various points on the rein, depending on how severe an action you wish to produce. The Market Harborough is allowed in national senior competitions in the UK as long as it is attached to a plain snaffle. Along with running and standing martingales these are the only aids permitted in the arena

The aim of the **Abbot Davies Balancing Rein** is to create the correct musculature for the horse to carry himself in a correct manner. It has three working positions, the first of which actually uses the horse's tail. The rein is attached to the horse's tail using a stretchable rubber fitting, travels under his belly, through pulleys attached to the bit ring, and clips to the reins.

It is intended to encourage the horse to engage his hindquarters to a greater extent, thus working on the front and back end of the horse. In the second position it attaches to the girth, again using the stretchable rubber fitting, runs through the pulleys and clips to the

**The Market Harborough**. When the horse is round, the Market Harborough is inactive.

If the horse begins to raise its head above the bit, the Market Harborough comes into play.

reins, and in the third position it is clipped to the poll. The latter position is mainly used for lungeing.

The Balancing Rein should be the rein of choice for the less experienced rider who may not be entirely balanced in the saddle and whose instinctive reactions are not quite as quick as they should be when things go wrong. It also limits the pulling power of the rider's hand so that the rider cannot be as lazy as he would like to be with his legs.

Although the Market Harborough is allowed in the arena I do not like to see it used by any but the most

experienced riders. If the rider is out of balance it can have a dramatically bad effect on the way a horse jumps.

### THE CHAMBON

This is a rein that I have always used with good effect on the lunge. As its name suggests, the Chambon was developed in France. The rein passes from the girth to a ring at the breast, where it splits in two and each rein then passes through two rings either side of the horse's poll to the bit rings. It acts on the horse's poll and his lips, not on the bars of the mouth. The theory behind

**The Abbot Davies Balancing Rein.** Inactive while the horse shows correct flexion.

The Abbot Davies rein begins to act as the horse raises its head above the bit.

**The de Gogue**. 'Command' position.

**The de Gogue**. 'Independent' position.

the Chambon is simplicity itself – if the horse raises his head, the pressure on the poll is increased; if he lowers his head, there is no pressure. Even the simplest horse works out very quickly that if he keeps his head lowered there is no pressure on his poll, and he is soon trotting around happily, stretching those all important back and neck muscles.

The main rules to remember when using the Chambon are:
• You should know your horse's temperament before you attempt to use it.
• It should be tightened carefully and by degrees.
• Only ever use the Chambon on the lunge, never when riding a horse.

For more information on using the Chambon, see Chapter 3, 'Lungeing the Show Jumper'.

### THE DE GOGUE

The de Gogue is a schooling rein developed from the Chambon and is designed to be used whilst the horse is being ridden. It can be used in two positions. In the passive or 'independent' position the rein passes from the girth to a ring at the breast, where the reins split into two. Each rein passes through a ring either side of the poll, through the bit rings and then returns to be clipped at the breast ring. In the active or 'command' position, once the reins have passed through the bit rings they travel directly to the rider's hands. In the passive position the de Gogue can be used on the lunge in very much the same manner as the Chambon. In the

active position the rider can use the de Gogue and because it is not fixed the rider can release the action of the rein if the horse reacts adversely to its pressure. Both positions have very much the same effect as the Chambon, working primarily on the horse's poll, and to a lesser extent on his lips, encouraging him to lower his head and engage his quarters, thus developing a strong topline.

### THE BUNGEE

I was given this rein, which originates in Poland, a few years ago. It is an elastic rein, which goes from the girth, through one bit ring, over the poll, through the other bit ring and returns to the girth. It has a similar effect to the Chambon but will give a little if the horse becomes upset by the pressure on the poll. It is therefore a rein that is safe to ride in.

## Boots

**Brushing boots**. There are many types of brushing boot and their purpose is to prevent the horse from damaging one leg by knocking it with another. They can be worn on front or hind legs.

**Tendon boots** (shown overleaf). Tendon boots are a modified type of brushing boot. They have reinforcement at the back and at either side of the tendon and are designed to support and protect the tendon, particularly when the horse is jumping or moving fast. They

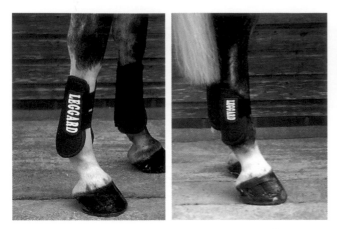

**Moulded tendon boots –** foreleg (shown above left) and hind (shown above right).

**Leather tendon boots** (above left) **and bell boots** with Velcro fastenings (above right).

are fitted only on the front legs.

**Bell boots or overreach boots** (shown above). These are fitted just above the coronary band on both front legs and protect the pastern and the balls of the heel, which might otherwise be struck by the hind feet. A few years ago these were notoriously difficult to put on as they were made of a continuous band of rubber and had to be pulled on over the hoof. The advent of velcro and other fastenings has meant that modern overreach boots are far easier to put in place.

## Studs

All showjumpers benefit from the use of studs fitted into their shoes. Studs give your horse's shoe more grip, thus enabling him to turn more safely and more

quickly. Different riders have different tastes. Some may have just one stud hole in the outside heel of each hind shoe (a practice that is no longer recommended as it is now thought to unbalance the foot), whereas I prefer to have two stud holes in each shoe, front and back. The type of stud you use will depend on the type of surface you are riding on. In deep mud you will want to use long, blunt studs, but on hard ground you will want to use short, sharp studs.

Different riders also have different ways of keeping their stud holes clean; some keep very small, blunt studs in the shoes at all times whereas others stuff the holes with cotton wool. Personally I use a bradawl to clean out the stud hole when I am ready to put my studs in. You will need a special tool called a stud tap to rebore the stud holes each time and to tighten the studs into the shoe. Try to keep all your studs clean and all the

**A selection of studs.** From left to right: soft ground to hard ground.

**A tidy stud box.**

**Fitting studs.** **(1)** Cleaning out the stud hole – a narrow screwdriver is good for this job. **(2)** Tapping out the stud hole – removing any dust and dirt whilst re-boring the thread of the stud hole. Note the square holes on the top of the tap which will be used to tighten up the stud in the hole. **(3)** Studs tightly screwed in the shoe.

Stud guard girth (on and off the horse).

equipment you will need tidy – there is nothing worse than not being able to find what you need when you need it.

Fitting studs can be a fiddly job so it might be an idea to practise and become proficient at home where you and your horse are calm and relaxed – once at a show your horse is likely to become akin to a kangaroo and you are likely to become a nervous wreck – all fingers and thumbs! You will also need to be careful when you are tightening the stud that you keep a firm grip of your horse's hoof. If he were to tread on the stud tap while it is in the hole it could either twist his fetlock or wrench off the shoe – either scenario will cause an abrupt and unwelcome end to your day!

**Stud guards.** Some horses are very tidy with their front legs and can even catch their belly with the studs in their front hooves. A stud guard is a specially shaped girth that protects the horse's belly from being pierced by studs.

# CHAPTER 21

# Management Tips for Show Jumpers

I n this chapter we look at some areas of horse care and management that are particularly relevant to the show jumper. Certainly, they are responsible for many of the common problems seen in this sport.

## Feeding

There are far too many overfed, overweight horses trying to compete on the show jumping circuit. So often a horse's bad behaviour and lack of progress stems directly from inappropriate feeding. The reasons for this are many, but most arise from bad and outmoded methods of stable management. If you are fighting the feed bin – that is, spending most of your time when riding trying to expend the excess energy that you have fed your horse – you are unlikely to make any progress either at home or at shows. To see jumping ponies being lunged for upwards of half an hour before they have settled down enough to accept a rider is quite a common but fundamentally unnecessary sight. Children's ponies do not need half a bucket of concentrates three times a day – in fact this is truly bad for them. Most ponies will compete happily off grass and good hay. Many feed companies now run help-lines to advise on correct feeding regimes. If you are not sure what to feed your horse, ring the experts!

Protein-rich feeds should not be given to show jumpers in large amounts; they tend to fare better on feeds that are high in fibre and carbohydrates, which will ultimately assist in muscle development. My own horses have a considerable amount of fibre; they have access to as much high quality, dust-free hay or haylage as they want. Many people now soak hay as a matter of course, ridding the hay of dry spores harmful to the horse's respiratory system. Haylage and silage are becoming more and more commonly used as a dust-free alternative.

Contamination by botulism is not uncommon if silage and haylage are not prepared and maintained correctly, and if ingested may prove fatal. If big-bale haylage is used, opened bales must be used within five days as harmful organisms begin to multiply after this time.

Whether you choose to feed hay, haylage or silage, it is imperative that the food you choose is of the best quality – if you do not know what you are looking for then make sure you have someone by your side who does. Poor quality fodder will at best be of no benefit to your horse and at worst will cause him serious, permanent damage.

## Fitness

All competition horses must be physically fit, but show jumpers do not have to push themselves to the extremes of physical exertion. Horses used purely for show jumping do not have to be 'racing' or even 'eventing' fit. These latter horses have to run as fast as they can for up to a quarter of an hour at a time. A show jumper has to produce an extreme burst of energy for an absolute maximum of three minutes at a time. Before you start to get your horse fit check his resting heart rate, resting respiratory rate, his normal temperature and keep a record of them. Firstly, these baseline observations will give you a physical indication of whether your horse is ever unwell, and secondly, you will find that as your horse becomes fitter his pulse and respiration rates will become slower.

To attain the degree of fitness necessary to compete you should first follow a simple fittening regime such as:

(1) a week at walk for half an hour
(2) a week of walk for an hour
(3) two weeks of walk and trot for an hour
(4) two weeks of walk, trot and canter for upwards of an hour

This is only necessary if the horse has had a prolonged holiday of say six or eight weeks, or has clearly never been fit before. Once your horse has achieved this level of fitness you can maintain it through the everyday work that you do with him – alternating schooling on the flat with work over jumps, hacking out, competing – and you can allow him the occasional day off in the field.

Remember that to perform well your horse has to be mentally fit as well as physically fit, and variety is important, but this should not be confused with inconsistency. Horses are creatures of habit and like to know what is likely to happen to them and when. Routine times for mucking out, feeding and riding will greatly reduce your horse's stress levels.

A two-week break (such as when you take your own summer holiday) is unlikely to affect your horse's general fitness as long as he is turned out or is allowed to stretch his legs on a horse walker each day. If you have a break from riding that is longer than two weeks it may be necessary to start your fitness programme again, although not necessarily from the beginning.

## Stable management system

Most professional show jumpers are stabled, day and night, through the year. It **is** possible to compete off the field but most riders do not have vast acreages and many feel that their horses concentrate on their jumping better if competed from the stable. Personally, I like my horses to spend as much of the summer in the paddock as possible, provided they do not become grossly overweight.

If you stable your horse then the quality of bedding you use is almost as important as the quality of fodder. There are now many types of bedding to choose from and which one you use will depend on cost, availability, and your method of disposal – and your horse. Good quality wheat straw is cheap, relatively easy to find and you may be able to entice the local mushroom grower into removing your muck heap for you. On the down side, some horses think that good quality wheat straw is really tasty and will gorge themselves on it. The other disadvantage is that, however good the quality of the straw, it will be a host to fungi and mould spores which will, in time, affect the horse's respiratory system.

Shredded paper, dust-extracted shavings and shredded hemp are all popular, dust-free bedding materials; and rubber matting is now often used to dramatically reduce bedding bills in the long term. It can be used completely on its own, although many people like to throw down a small amount of shavings to absorb splash and moisture from urine.

Whatever bedding you decide to use and whatever method of mucking out you employ – full mucking out once or twice a day, semi deep litter or total deep litter – the same golden rules apply: the bed should be deep

**Safe turn-out.** These horses are enjoying a spell of summer grazing in well-fenced paddocks.

**Shredded hemp** is a highly absorbent bedding that is labour-saving, if properly managed.

**Wood shavings** make comfortable, dust-free beds that are relatively easy to maintain.

**Shredded paper beds** are dust- and spore-free, and therefore good for horses with dust allergies.

enough that the horse cannot feel the underlying ground surface, and dry enough that he does not become damp when lying down.

A horse that is stabled should be ridden, or at least able to stretch his legs somehow, at least once a day. The best method of doing this is to turn out into a safe, grassed paddock, but if you have no grazing then turning out into a schooling area or exercising on a horse walker is totally acceptable. Horse walkers are the boon of many big stables, enabling several horses to be exercised at one time.

## Looking after your horse's back

The act of jumping puts a great amount of strain on your horse's physical structure. The explosive action of take-off exerts immense pressure on your horse's spine and hindquarters, and the impact of landing sends considerable forces from the hoof, through the front legs and the shoulder to the wither and, again, through the spine. Injuries commonly associated with show jumpers include front tendon problems (especially in puissance horses) and muscle stiffness through the withers and in the saddle area.

Specialist equine physiotherapy is a relatively new phenomenon but it has proved an invaluable tool for keeping show jumpers fit and flexible.

If your horse is competing on an infrequent basis and is used mainly for hacking you should have his back examined and treated by a physiotherapist once or preferably twice a year. However, if you are competing on a regular basis you should have him checked at least once a month, and if a specific problem is identified, weekly visits may be necessary.

One way to minimise the risk of injury to your horse is through passive stretches. These simple stretches are best carried out after your horse has been ridden, when his muscles are warm. If your horse is not in work, due to injury or time off, you can still carry out the stretches, but make sure that you increase the pressure on the muscles **very gradually** so as not to cause tissue damage. Stretches may be particularly helpful if you have been jumping on hard ground.

Here are six passive stretches that will help the jumping horse:

**Horse-walker in action.** These exercisers can be a great asset in a busy yard.

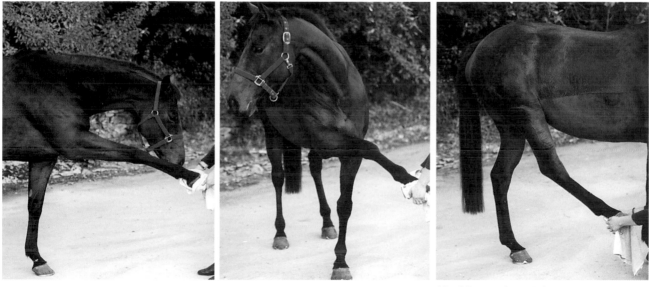

Forward stretch.

Lateral stretch.

Hind forward stretch.

## The forward stretch

Stand directly in front of your horse and place your hands around your horse's front hoof with the little fingers supporting the ball of the foot. Lift his leg forward and gradually use your weight as a counter balance against your horse's weight, thus stretching his leg forward. Once you feel that your horse is comfortably at the limit of his range, hold the stretch for twenty seconds, then gradually release the pressure on the leg and move the leg back to standing position. Repeat the exercise with the other foreleg.

This stretch creates maximum length and flexibility in your horse's front tendons, through his front leg, up into his shoulder and withers. It is particularly useful for short striding horses.

## The lateral stretch

This stretch starts just as the forward stretch above, but as your horse reaches the limit of the stretch, you move sideways in front of him so that he crosses his foreleg. Again, stretch the leg to its comfortable limit and count to twenty. Relax the leg and gently return it to standing position.

This stretch will increase your horse's looseness and flexibility. It helps to free the upper and lower shoulder areas and is particularly beneficial for your lateral work, e.g. leg yielding and half-pass.

## The hind forward stretch

This stretch is carried out in much the same manner as the forward stretch, but on the hind legs. Your horse will find this stretch more difficult and may pull his leg violently backwards. Proceed with patience and caution. As you are now at your horse's side, be careful that you do not get pulled under your horse; just gently pick up the hind leg again and start afresh. After stretching for twenty seconds gently return the leg to the standing position and repeat with the other hind leg.

## The quarters stretch (shown overleaf)

This exercise starts in the same manner as the hind forward stretch, but as your horse's hind leg reaches its comfortable forward limit, you take a couple of small paces backwards and lift the leg towards your horse's belly, to its comfortable upwards limit. Hold the position for twenty seconds before carrying out the same exercise on the other hind leg.

The hind forward stretch and the quarters stretch are particularly useful for horses that display signs of stiffness through the spine and hindquarters, and also for horses with arthritic hocks.

## The lateral neck stretch (shown overleaf)

The neck stretch is usually enjoyed by your horse because it involves titbits. Using a tempting morsel, such

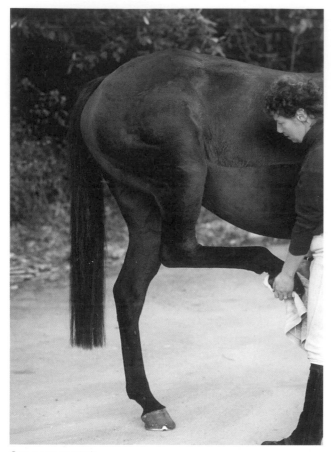

Quarters stretch.

Lateral neck stretch.

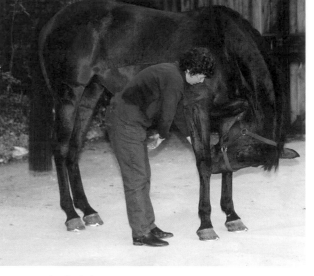

Lower neck stretch.

as a piece of carrot, encourage your horse to bend his head backwards towards his flank before giving him the piece of carrot. Until your horse becomes used to this exercise you will need to have the opposing side against a wall as he will attempt to reach the carrot by just walking around you in a circle. Once your horse becomes more adept at lateral neck stretches you can ask him to stretch for longer periods of time, and you can hold the carrot further and further back towards his haunches.

Lateral neck stretches help to loosen and strengthen the muscles in the shoulder and throughout the neck.

## Lower neck stretches

In this exercise you hold a piece of carrot or other titbit between your horse's front legs, encouraging him to lower his neck and head. Once he is comfortable with the exercise you can increase the degree of difficulty by holding the carrot lower and further back between his front legs, and asking him to stretch for longer periods of time.

This exercise helps to stretch the muscles in the top of your horse's neck and also all along the topline of his spine – an area likely to become tense and congested through jumping.

# Riding surfaces

### SAND

Sand used to be the only type of artificial surface that riders would meet in the arena; now there are many and I like **all** of them! My favourite, and the type I use at home, is shredded rubber laid on top of silica sand. It provides the horse with a good shock-absorbing surface and gives plenty of grip. It can be used equally well for jumping and flat work, and is usable in all extremes of weather (other than six inches of snow!). It is also long lasting and environmentally friendly.

Vaseline-coated PVC granules mixed with silica sand is another durable, all-weather surface that is very popular with riders. It has many of the same values as the rubber riding surface, but in an outdoor situation is more likely to bleed into the surrounding area unless fairly high boundary boards are used.

PVC granules and sand makes quite a useful surface if you do not want to jump too high or turn too fast – it has a tendency to slip if too dry. It is long-lasting but does need topping up regularly to prevent damage to the water-porous membrane underneath.

Synthetic fibre and sand is another good surface for most types of riding, as long as it is damp. If it is too dry the fibre and the sand tend to lift up, separate and fly away. For jumping, this surface can be a little on the 'dead' side and is not very forgiving on horses' legs. It does need quite a lot of maintenance and can freeze, but it does drain well.

### WOOD BARK

Wood bark and hardwood chips are not very durable and are prone to freezing, therefore they are not a first choice in any arena.

### GRASS

Grass is obviously the most natural of riding surfaces. At its best there is nothing better to ride on – it is springy and the horses do not slip on it. At its worst grass is slippery and sticky, but you should learn to ride on any type of surface. There is a very simple rule about riding on slippery going – you must remain balanced. Horses generally slip through lack of confidence. Horses full of confidence place their feet down firmly and positively and will jump out of the worst going. As soon as you start pushing and pulling and taking your horse out of balance he will not go so well, so stay calm and in balance and do not over-compensate for the conditions.

It is definitely possible to improve grass surfaces – look at Hickstead, which year after year presents riders with beautiful going whatever the weather conditions, but rather than accosting Douglas Bunn and asking him how to do it, go out and buy yourself a good gardening book!

# CHAPTER 22

# Horses Behaving Badly

Sometimes we encounter problems in our riding and handling - not all horses are saints, and neither are we! My advice is always to seek professional help, but here are a few ideas for dealing with some everyday problems.

## Rushing and refusing

Here, the term 'rushing' is not referring to the exuberant horse who bounds confidently towards his fences with a bright eye and his ears pricked, but rather the sorry animal racing flat-out at a fence with his ears flat back against his skull. Horses don't run towards things, they run away from them; so if you have a horse who is rushing towards his fences you have to ask yourself: how did it start, and when did it start?

Did it start because you chased your horse to his fences, through your own lack of confidence? Probably. If you ride him this way often enough he begins to think this is how you want him to behave, so he starts running at his fences. The trouble is that he is now coming into his fences in a flat, unbalanced stride, and before long he will frighten himself by crashing through them rather than clearing them.

Horses have a tremendously good memory for pain and a fairly low pain threshold: once a horse has hurt himself trying to jump a fence he will remember the experience for a very long time. Often the outcome is that he will start to stop at or run past fences at the end of his headlong gallop towards them.

So, refusals stem from a lack of confidence. Solution? Go back to basics.

Firstly, if the rider's lack of confidence is at the root of the problem then he must either gain confidence through coaching and experience or give the ride of the horse to a more confident jockey.

Secondly, because the horse has learned to rush or refuse habitually, he must now learn the habit not to rush or stop. You can teach him to do this in the following ways:

- you can come quietly around the corner towards the fence and then pull up to a walk, and walk towards the fence, halting in front of it; repeat this exercise five, ten or twenty times until he is calm, then allow the horse to jump the fence;

- you can make a circle on the approach line – again, circle five, ten or fifteen times and jump the fence only once.

- you can put trotting poles in front of the fence to regulate the horse's pace, and progress to canter poles;

> *Points to ponder…*
> * *Horses generally do as they are told – they are often told to do the wrong things.*

- you can teach your horse to collect and extend his canter, slow and increase his tempo.

Whatever method you choose to re-educate your horse it will only work if you have the confidence to carry your plans through.

## Rearing

Horses do not rear because they enjoy it. They do it because they are not happy – either physically or mentally. Is your horse unhappy due to a sore mouth (ulcers?), a sharp tooth, a pinching bit, a sore back, a pinching girth or an ill-fitting saddle? The first place to look for clues is your tack and what is underneath it. Another cause could be fear or uncertainty – see also Napping below.

If your horse does rear, transfer your weight forward, lower one hand to the level of your knee and ask your horse to turn using that rein. Once he comes back down to earth continue to ask him to turn in a small circle, at a gentle walk, for a couple of minutes. Once he is calm, dismount and try to ascertain the reasons for the rear. **Do not** try to bring your horse over backwards. You, your horse and your saddle are precious and easily broken in such a circumstances and I would strongly advise everybody to steer clear of this tactic – I have yet to hear of it 'curing' a rearer anyway.

An habitual rearer – one who appears to rear for no other reason than to try and dislodge his rider – is a very rare beast indeed. However, such horses do exist and what is going on in their tortured minds we will never know. Sadly, such horses tend to be incurable and should be disposed of humanely.

## Napping

One cause of napping (which can also apply to rearing) is that of fear and uncertainty. In the yard, the horse feels secure and comfortable; he has all his equine friends around him and he knows where and what everything is. Suddenly, there you are, taking your horse out of the gate, away from his familiar surroundings and venturing into the big unknown. If your horse has had an unpleasant experience 'out there' he will not want to try it again.

To begin with, he just does not want to move forward. The next stage is that he refuses to go forward, and then, when you spur him or whip him to make him move forward, he goes up on his hind legs. Punishing the horse in such circumstances is only likely to confirm his suspicions that 'out there' is not a good place to be. That is not to say that you should not use the whip at all – sometimes the whip has the desired effect of instantly focusing the horse's mind on something else other than his desire to stay where he is; but if one crack of the whip has no effect, a beating will only cause bigger problems.

In these circumstances you must try to break the chain at the beginning. Start by walking him a short way with another, familiar horse. Make your trips longer each time and begin to take different routes. Eventually the horse should be happy to leave the yard on his own.

Napping outside the jumping arena has much the same roots. You are asking your horse to leave all his friends and to go and do some work; either the horse is green and is frightened of what might happen, or he is an old pro who knows exactly what is going to happen and doesn't much fancy it! The green horse needs reassurance and good experiences; the older horse needs taking back to basics and re-schooling.

## Bucking

Horses tend to buck either because they are happy or too fresh. Often the most simple cure for bucking is work or a turn out in the paddock. Frequently the cause of a horse's freshness is not just lack of work but also over-feeding. If your horse doesn't stop bucking when given less food and more work then the problem may be, as with rearing, discomfort. Again, check your horse for sites of pain and your tack for signs of poor fitting.

Kicking back is different from bucking. If a horse persistently kicks back a stride or two after the jump I would be suspicious that it has something wrong with its spine and would probably consult a chiropractor or physiotherapist.

## Bolting

Being on top of a horse that is bolting is a terrifying experience. The horse is running blindly ahead with no concern for his own safety, let alone yours. There is absolutely nothing you can do other than hope that he will soon run out of steam. Pulling on one rein usually just pulls the bit through the horse's mouth, but if you are in a ten-acre field it may eventually bring the horse onto a circle and if this happens, you can keep reducing the size of your circle until the horse comes to a stop.

I would consider jumping off a bolting horse only if we were heading for a busy road – other than that you are probably safer on top.

## Running through the bridle

A horse that is running through the bridle is not bolting, but the experience is just as worrying for the rider. Often the horse doesn't even realise that he is out of control – only the rider knows that. Basically, the horse is totally aware of what he is doing and usually his plan is to get back to his stable as quickly as possible. Again, the best plan is to try and get the horse onto a circle and then to reduce its velocity and diameter.

## Shying

All horses shy whether young or old, although some appear to be more spooky than others. I do not punish horses for shying – I ignore it or turn the horse's head away from whatever object he is shying at. Habitual shying whilst on the road can be dangerous, so if I had a horse that I knew was particularly spooky I would avoid roadwork with him.

*Points to ponder...*

- *Bad tempers don't win arguments.*

## Kicking and biting

Years ago I was told that if I got bitten or kicked I was in the wrong place! Not very sympathetic, but nearly always true.

Horses are territorial animals, some more so than others, and they like their own space. If you invade that space without the horse's assent you are likely to get kicked or bitten.

The feeding of titbits on a regular basis is likely to train a horse to bite, so don't do it! I was also told that the best way to respond to a horse that had bitten or kicked me was to bite or to kick it back! It can work, but not many people are prepared to leap on a horse and bite his ear!

Some horses just don't like other horses, and some horses are horrendously bad-tempered in the stable but shining stars in the ring – it is a fact we have to accept and have to respond to.

If your horse bites, tie him short so he can't get to you, other horses or other people with his teeth. If he kicks, avoid his back legs, and if you are going to pick up his back feet stand as close to his side as you can to minimise his movement and length of swing.

If you know that your horse is likely to kick, you should tie a red ribbon around his tail – carefully! You should also, out of courtesy, inform other riders if your horse is likely to bite or kick them or their mounts.

## Stable vices

Stable vices, such as weaving, wind sucking, crib-biting and box walking, nearly always stem from boredom. Keeping a horse in a stable or even in a field on his own twenty-four hours a day will create boredom, and a bored horse will begin to find different ways of relieving the tedium.

To prevent your horse from developing bad habits, keep him occupied. Ride him regularly, take him to competitions, turn him out frequently, and when you have no access to a paddock ensure that somebody is in the yard frequently to provide interest, and provide him with 'toys', such as a mineral lick or a swede on a rope suspended from the middle of the stable door.

*Happy show jumping!*

# Index